Seducing Strangers

Seducing Strangers

How to Get People to Buy
What You're Selling

{The Little Black Book of Advertising Secrets}

Josh Weltman

Workman Publishing
New York

For Angela

Library of Congress Cataloging-in-Publication Data is available.

ISBNs 978-0-7611-8175-0 (pb); 978-0-7611-8495-9 (hc)

Design by Jean-Marc Troadec

Workman books are available at special discounts when purchased in bulk for premiums and sales promotions as well as for fund-raising or educational use. Special editions or book excerpts also can be created to specification. For details, contact the Special Sales Director at the address below, or send an email to specialmarkets@workman.com.

WORKMAN PUBLISHING COMPANY, INC.
225 VARICK STREET
NEW YORK, NY 10014-4381
workman.com

Printed in the United States of America
First printing March 2015

10 9 8 7 6 5 4 3 2 1

Contents

Foreword by Jon Hamm

Josh Weltman is the unsung hero of *Mad Men.* Beyond the clothes, the women, the booze and cigarettes, Josh provides our world with a credible foundation in an industry that exists, almost by definition, in an incredible, or at least hyperbolic, state.

Don Draper is actually good at his job because Josh is actually good at his. Josh's former career and wealth of experience as an actual creative director making actual campaigns to sell *actual things* has brought authenticity, depth, and resonance to this character who thinks and creates for a living. This contribution has been invaluable to the whole of the character and to the story.

People often ask me questions or ask my opinions on or about the world of advertising. My stock response is "You know I play a *fictional* advertising executive, right?" That's usually used to cover the ignorance or stupidity of whatever I am about to say next. In the future, I will simply refer them to Josh.

Seducing Strangers

Introduction
The Job That Was Once Called Advertising

The job was using words, pictures, stories, and music to make someone somewhere do something. In the industrial, mass-media, consumer economy of the past, the job was called advertising, and "Mad men" did it. In our modern, service-based, social-media-centric information economy, the job is called life, and everybody does it.

Once it was the job of these advertising executives on Madison Avenue—"Mad men"—to be the public champions of products and services, making businesses successful and customers happy. Don Draper always seemed to know exactly how to do it. He knew what the business goal of the advertising was. He knew how to create an insightful, persuasive message. And he had teams of experts to help him decide which media would help him do the job best.

In today's information economy, the power to persuade remains the coin of the realm. But persuasion is no longer the job of just a creative director and a host of media buyers. Today it's everyone's job. People working in today's information economy spend all or most of their time and effort trying to get someone somewhere to do something. From the CEO of a multinational company trying to establish a presence on Facebook to a teenager tweeting about a pair of awesome-looking jeans, everyone needs to be able to effectively persuade someone, whether it's a boss or a boyfriend, a customer or a committee.

The problem is that most people today don't feel equipped to craft messages or take action with the same confidence and certainty as *Mad Men*'s Don Draper. Two things confound them. First, most are a lot less familiar with the *principles* of persuasion than they are with the means. They're not quite sure what makes a message persuasive, but they know how to use a smartphone to tweet 140 characters to millions of people in a second. Second, recent and rapid changes in new digital media technology make doing the job hard—even for experts who *do* understand the principles of persuasion. Why? Because today there are more ways to go about it than ever. Changes in media affect how we figure out the "somewhere" part of the job. And with all the hype, hysteria, big money, high-tech IPOs, consolidation, disruption, and destruction that is the digital media revolution, people who are trying to get someone somewhere to do something can lose sight of the "get someone" and the "do something" part of the job.

Lee Clow is president and chief creative officer of TBWA/Media Arts Lab. The man behind acclaimed multimedia ad campaigns for Apple, Nissan, Energizer Battery, and Pedigree Petfoods, among others, Clow is arguably the most famous and acclaimed creative director ever. This is what he said recently when asked about the current state of advertising:

"We haven't come close to figuring out how to use all these new-media opportunities, and most clients are very conflicted about what media they should use, why, and how. They keep thinking there's some new silver bullet in the new-media world that will allow them to save money or find a new way to twist consumers' arms."

This book establishes some new communications principles to help you come up with more effective, persuasive ideas and understand where to place them in a world of changing technology and changing consumer expectations.

I never would have written this book if I had not been hired to be an advertising consultant on *Mad Men*. My job was to see that the show accurately depicted the process of creating ads and servicing clients. I didn't know what I knew about advertising or how I did it until I needed to explain it to *Mad Men* creator Matt Weiner and the show's writing and production staff.

In the writers' room, Matt would constantly ask me and Bob Levinson, the show's other advertising consultant, "What would they *do* in this situation?" Weiner and the other writers were trying to make drama, not advertising. He wasn't interested in what was going through Don's head when Don stared out the window. He was interested only in what could be seen, said, and dramatized and how it made the story better, more intriguing or surprising.

Seven years spent thinking about how to depict the process of persuasion made me think deeply about what I do to create and sell ideas that connect with and motivate other people. It made me think a lot about what is principle and what is fashion. What was it about getting someone somewhere to do something that would have been as true in the midcentury *Mad Men* world of Madison Avenue as it is today? And what ideas about advertising were just 1960s style?

Today every Starbucks I walk into looks like every creative department I've ever been in. People are writing, creating presentations, blogging, and trying to think of ideas to tweet, email, or post in order to persuade someone somewhere to do something. My aim here is to offer some proven techniques that have helped me do the same things—faster, better, and more confidently.

The goal of this book is to explain how messages that make people do things *work*. And it's written for anyone expected to make something happen by using words, pictures, stories, or music.

To help me understand a client's goals, I often ask, "It's a year from now, and we've all come back into this conference room to celebrate the success of this ad campaign we've created. Tell me, what are we celebrating? What did we do? What happened? How did we know when it was time to stop working and open a bottle of Champagne?"

A year from now, I want to walk into a Starbucks and see someone sitting at a table with a computer and a couple of books. One is a Moleskine notebook. It's filled with ideas, sketches, headlines, scraps of paper, bits and pieces. The other is a copy of this book. It's dog-eared and worn. The spine is cracked. Passages are underlined, and bookmarks are sticking out all over it. And the person sitting at that table with his laptop and books has that "Please don't talk to me. I need to get this idea down before I lose it" look.

When I see that, I'll know I've done my job, and I'll open a bottle of Champagne.

This book is for anyone expected to make something happen by using words, pictures, stories, or music.

Part One
The Secret Purpose of Advertising

"When I get asked…'What's the secret to success?'
I just say: 'Early to bed, early to rise, work like hell,
and advertise.'"

—Ted Turner at Montana State
University–Northern, 2011

The Job of Advertising Is to Make People Happy

Happiness occurs when expectations are met or exceeded by reality.

Unfortunately, people, companies, and organizations are not always good at setting expectations for their own products, services, or offerings. That's why they need the likes of us. Talented artists, sensitive writers, agents, designers, barkers, promoters, performers, bloggers, pitchmen, and adwomen to help individuals and companies make people happy by setting customers' expectations at a level their products and services can meet or exceed.

The job of a persuader is to make promises that motivate, sell, and seduce. These promises are kept by the actions, products, or services of others. It's a tango for two.

Persuading is about getting someone to do your will. Selling is about making your proposition, goods, or services attractive, visible, and well priced. Yet there's no way around it: To achieve certain business goals, companies and organizations—and the people who do the manufacturing, measuring, and managing—need to get *emotional*. That's where seduction comes in. Seduction takes both sensitivity and insight. Seduction is about listening to customers and understanding their feelings, wants, needs, and motives. It's understanding what people desperately want to hear about themselves and telling them just that.

To successfully do the job of persuading, selling to, and seducing strangers, talented folks use insight, words, pictures, stories, and music to evoke emotions that motivate people they don't know for the benefit of people, companies, and organizations that don't know how.

Does Advertising Work?

People ask me all the time, "Does advertising work?" These are smart people, people who would never dream of asking an engineer, "Does engineering work?" or asking a doctor, "Does medicine work?" This year, in the United States alone, companies will spend $140 billion on advertising. I believe the people spending those dollars get something for their money. But before you can say whether or not advertising works, you need to know what its job is. What's the goal of advertising? What is it supposed to do? How can you say whether it works or doesn't if you don't know what it's supposed to achieve?

I've worked with people who think the purpose of advertising is to build businesses. Others expect it to build brands. No matter the philosophy, effective advertising is made up of communications, messages, videos, stories, posts, blog entries, or tweets that get the intended audience to do what the people sending the message want them to do. Different people come to the endeavor with all kinds of different expectations. They do different jobs and have different motives, personality types, processes, beliefs, business goals, ideas, and expectations. A good place to start getting someone somewhere to do something is by zeroing in on exactly what the people doing the getting want to get.

Just about everyone has heard of a miserable rich person. Likewise, many of us know a happy poor person. In fact, happiness isn't really about what people do or don't have. It's about what they *expect* to have and how well those expectations match up with reality.

Advertising is one of the most effective ways for businesses to establish customer expectations. And when a company sets a level of anticipation that its products or services meet or exceed, it creates happy customers.

No advertising equals no expectations. No expectations equals no exceeded expectations. No exceeded expectations equals no happy customers.

Take Google Glass, those eyeglasses with the little device on the side. Now, I spend a good part of my income on high-tech products and consider myself an early adopter. Yet I have no idea why I need Google Glass to improve my life. Can I see what time a movie starts by using Google Glass to look at a theater? Can I see if the person I'm talking to has ever been arrested? Can I look at the street and find the quickest path to an ATM or a bathroom? I can't imagine what Google Glass is all about. And I shouldn't have to. Google may have invented something really great but has failed to make me curious enough about the product to check it out. This is a perfect example of an "over the wall" mentality.

> No advertising equals no expectations. No expectations equals no exceeded expectations. No exceeded expectations equals no happy customers.

Although Google gets it right most of the time, some companies, like some people, are just not that great at connecting with others. High-tech companies are notorious for spending large amounts of money to develop and create wonderful products, then "throwing them over the wall"—that is, neglecting to support them with enough advertising and marketing dollars to create buyer expectations before bringing them to market.

I imagine the practice of throwing things over the wall is rooted in the idea that if you build a better mousetrap, the world will beat a path to your door. But better is subjective. What constitutes a person's expectations for a better mousetrap? A quieter one? A bigger one? A less painful one? Any one of these promises could be compelling to someone in the market for a mousetrap. "Better" is in the mind of the person who's buying the mousetrap, not the person building it. If you come up with an innovative idea for a new mousetrap but fail to advertise or communicate why it will forever change what people expect from a mousetrap, you're going to miss out on a lot of customers—not to mention end up with a warehouse full of mousetraps.

> "Better" is in the mind of the person who's buying the mousetrap, not the person · building it.

Build a better mousetrap and advertise the hell out of it. Then the world will beat a path to your door. And go away happy.

The Truth About Liars

Everyone thinks ads and advertisers lie. Successful ones don't. There are three reasons why.

1. **Lying is bad for business.** The great and oft-quoted Bill Bernbach, founder and creative director of Doyle Dane Bernbach, once said, "Nothing kills a bad product faster than good advertising." He meant that if you get out there with a compelling promise and the product fails to live up to expectations, it's doomed. Fifty years later, with Yelp, Facebook, and other social media in the world, communicators would be crazy to knowingly lie. Make a good promise for a bad product and customer disappointment will get around fast. Make a good promise for a bad product to people connected by social media and watch business implode at the speed of light.

2. **The truth is far more compelling than a good lie.** Before the first season of *Mad Men* began, I was talking with showrunner Matt Weiner about what it's like to work in an advertising agency. The movies and TV shows I'd seen about advertising didn't exactly lie about what it's like to create ads, but they didn't tell the truth either. I explained the difference between a TV creative department and a real one by telling Matt that on TV it always looked like the ad folks actually created solutions to clients' problems. Ideas would just

pop into their heads. They looked brilliant. In twenty-five years of working in creative departments, I never once felt I was *creating* the answer to a problem. For me, the solution always felt like a process of discovery, not invention. Like the answer was out there, waiting to be found. It always came down to understanding what consumers really wanted. What was going to make them *happy*?

I would be lying if I said I thought of myself—or any of the really good ad people I've worked with—as particularly creative. The truth is, I think good ad people are very curious. They're fascinated by what motivates people—and they're much more insightful than creative.

Discovering the one thing that makes customers tick that no one else has ever figured out is what ad agencies refer to as the consumer insight, and it's the single most important element in the development of effective communication.

The discovery of a consumer insight was illustrated nicely on the episode of *Mad Men* in which the agency is working on a lipstick assignment. The company wanted to promote the large selection of colors it offered. But the young secretary, Peggy Olson, pointed out something far more compelling and true: No woman wants to be just another color in a box. A woman wants her lipstick to be *her* color.

Another example of the real truth being more powerful than a good lie was illustrated in a schematic I brought with me the first day I was invited into the *Mad Men* writers' room. In the corner of one chart, titled Agency Point of View, I wrote a little note that spoke to the customer's opinion about truth and advertising. It read:

> Consumer insight is the single most important element of effective communication.

Frightening: *There are big multinational corporations out there spending billions of dollars to get me to buy crap that leaves me broke and feeling empty.*

More frightening: *There is something inside me that I can't control that compels me to buy crap that leaves me broke and feeling empty.*

The second insight is more frightening because it's truer. People are driven to act by their own impulses far more often than by outside forces. Advertising is not about changing their beliefs or the things that drive them. It's about *confirming* them.

Take the example of L'Oréal hair color and its slogan: "Because you're worth it." What woman hasn't felt the need for a little reward after a tough day at work, an afternoon with a screaming child, or a dispute with a problem partner? The itch for gratification is already there. L'Oréal or Godiva chocolates or Kate Spade is just helping her scratch it. Nobody needs to lie about how rewarding a product is or isn't. You just need to remind people who feel they deserve a reward that they are absolutely right to feel that way.

The job of any good persuader is figuring out what people want and what motivates them to make the choices they make—in other words, finding the urge that lies within and poking it to wake it up. Effective persuasion leverages people's inherent beliefs. It doesn't change or control them.

Advertising is not mind control. It's not about making people want stuff they don't want, or do things they don't want to do. It's mostly about persuading people to do a little more of what they're already doing.

What's more, so much time and effort is spent by

> People are driven to act by their own impulses far more often than by outside forces.

communicators doing research and looking for that compulsive thing inside people that motivates them to buy one thing over another, that if and when it's found, the last thing an advertiser would ever need or want to do is lie about it.

3. **Self-interest tends to keep advertising people from lying.** If they are dishonest about what really motivates a person to buy things, the ads simply won't work. And that's bad for their careers.

The advertising industry talks a lot about imagination and constantly celebrates creativity. But along with creativity, the successful ad people I've met and worked with share four essential traits: they are all keen observers, good listeners, endlessly curious—and they all have an almost pathological inability to lie about human nature. These are smart and calculating businessmen and businesswomen. They are the ones who call bullshit when something doesn't ring true. And the reason they call bullshit is to protect their livelihoods.

Most people don't trust the stuff that's coming out of the television, the Internet, or just about anywhere, but all of them believe that what they feel inside is true. That's what the phrase "the customer is always right" is really all about. Even in the face of overwhelming evidence to the contrary, people will rarely change their beliefs about what is true. And it pays to respect that. I tend to back away from projects if I hear clients or agency people explain a communication strategy by saying, "We need to educate the public" or "We need to change people's minds." Or my favorite, the one I hear every week on the Sunday morning talk shows, "We need to change the way society thinks about" whatever. Good luck with that. I don't sign

> Advertising is not mind control. It's not about making people want stuff they don't want, or do things they don't want to do. It's mostly about persuading people to do a little more of what they're already doing.

on to do campaigns that are determined to alter the way people think, because I do what I do in order to make a living, and there's not a lot of money in telling people they're wrong and need to come around. The money is in telling people they're right and to keep on doing what they're doing—preferably with your particular brand, product, or service.

It was very important to Matt Weiner from Day One that Don Draper be good at his job, because it was the one thing about this flawed character that the audience could really like. For me, that led to the main insight into the character and the most important conceit of the show: Don Draper can lie anywhere, *except* in the advertising.

You're Brought In to Back Off

As counterintuitive as it seems, the people designing, manufacturing, and distributing products and services—those who know the stuff inside and out—are often too close to their products, services, and businesses to see how they fit into the bigger picture of other people's lives.

I discovered the benefits of backing off in my first life-drawing class at the Brentwood Art Center. The instructor gave every student a three-by-four-foot pad of cheap newsprint and a piece of red chalk fastened to the end of a two-foot stick. He then positioned the model and told the class to back away from our pads, extend our arms straight out, and begin to draw her using only our shoulders. He wanted us to learn how to draw big shapes with our shoulders, then smaller shapes with our elbows and wrists, and finally details with our hands and fingers. Standing about four feet away from our pads, with our arms rigid and our chalk at the end of a stick, we looked more like fencers than artists.

We all started swinging our straight arms from our shoulders, slashing at our newsprint like drunken sword fighters. Without using elbows, wrists, or fingers, all you can manage to draw are big shapes. I made one big mass to represent the model's torso. Another clump of scribbles showed where the head should be. And I drew straight, heavy, vertical lines to indicate where the model was putting her weight.

After two minutes of this, we ripped off the sheet of newsprint, the model took a new pose, and we began again.

By the end of the class, we were standing up to our waists in crumpled newsprint. The drawings looked like scribbled garbage; nothing I took home that day looked anything like a live human being. But that wasn't the point.

The point was to teach us how to see the shapes and masses and forces that formed the pose. We were learning how to stand back and see what a pose was made of before trying to draw it. That day, I had looked at and seen a body in a way I'd never seen one before. Before that class, when I had looked at a body, I saw what I knew. I saw a bunch of parts that had names, like legs and nose and head and arms. And I tried to draw what I knew. That day, I saw the pose as made up of things I did not know. As I swung my chalk on a stick and used broad strokes, I could mark down on the paper only the big things with no names that were unique to the pose—the masses and tensions and weights and shadows and folds of flesh that were part of neither the leg nor the torso. I saw only what was actually in front of me, not what I thought to be there.

The need to back away to see the big picture more clearly came up throughout my career in advertising, and then again when I started working on *Mad Men*.

At the beginning of every season, Matt Weiner would assemble a team of eight to twelve writer/producers, executive producers, and advertising consultants to basically listen to him talk for a couple of days. He'd talk about the big picture: what he felt was going on with the main characters, what was happening in the country during each season's time frame, and how it was relevant to people's current lives.

Then everyone would go away to think. We'd take some time to step back and see what kinds of shapes would emerge.

A few days later, we'd come back to the table with ten ideas that we would take turns reading aloud. Some of the ideas were thematic, others were simply words or images. One writer might have a fully fleshed-out story; another might contribute a good-size chunk of a story in need of an ending. We'd finish the day by writing a couple of words to indicate each idea on three-by-five-inch cards that we pinned to a wall.

Those cards contained the issues, themes, motives, images, and forces that would eventually become fourteen forty-seven-minute episodes, or an entire television season. As with my art class, we began each season of the show concentrating on the big masses and forces before trying to render the specifics.

This was illustrated in "Waterloo," episode 7 of the seventh season of *Mad Men,* which was centered on the first manned lunar landing, which took place on July 20, 1969. We started out by asking ourselves general questions like "What was the significance of going to the moon? What did it mean? Was it about an incredible engineering feat, or a bigger issue like striving or discovery or something even more personal?" It took us about a week to step back and watch the shape of the season reveal itself.

The pivotal episode focused on how the event was experienced from different characters' points of view. For Sally Draper, it was about the romance of the moon and how it led up to her first kiss under the stars. For Bert Cooper, who dies shortly after witnessing the moon walk, it's about the culmination of personal achievement. Bert spent his life acquiring and achieving, and as he witnesses the ultimate triumph of mankind, he feels complete. And for Peggy Olson and Don Draper, who watch the landing together in a hotel room on the night before a big presentation, it's about what people can achieve when they work together.

You need to see what the problem is made of before trying to solve it.

The writers' room on *Mad Men* was different from other recent endeavors I've been part of because we took time to step back and contemplate. Unfortunately, this is not often possible in today's fast-moving, narrowly focused business world. Yet what often looks like wasting time is an essential—and valuable—part of the creative process.

Helping busy clients step back and gain perspective is part of every good persuader's job. Clients may know the names of all the parts of their business they're dealing with, like product components and sales figures, but they may not be able to see the shapes and forces affecting the market that are right there in front of them, whether it's the changing social landscape or consumers thinking twice about buying luxury items today.

I've found that what works well for drawing and screenwriting works with just about every type of persuasive communication. When thinking about a communications problem, try staring at it for a few minutes.

> You need to see what the problem is made of before trying to solve it.

Then break it down into themes, phrases, or the basic pieces you have to work with. The answer will often come from looking at the parts and putting them together in a new and different way.

As Don Draper explains to Peggy, "Fill your head with all the information you can. Then go to the movies." What he means is that it's virtually impossible to think about the big and small picture at the same time. You need to let your subconscious help you work on the big picture and general shapes.

Next time you get a creative assignment, don't stop staring into space or taking those long walks. It's exactly what you need in order to back off—and get closer to a solution.

Do You Want to Sell or Seduce?

Businesses often want to communicate or sell the tangible features of the products and services they provide—like the lightweight, breathable fabric of a shirt. But customers mostly buy the ephemeral benefits they want—soft, cozy, comfort. When customers buy stuff, it's not really about the stuff itself, rather it's about *them.* I prefer the word *people* to *consumers* or *customers.* It reminds me that when people buy stuff, they're always buying something personal. They're buying an item for the way it benefits them.

I stopped selling and started seducing when I understood the difference between the tangible features companies *sell* and the ephemeral benefits people *buy.* I was first struck by this insight in the early 1990s, when my writing partner, Chris Boutée, and I were working on a new TV campaign for Doritos. As part of our preparation, we attended focus groups with the people who ate the product most: teenagers.

Until we started working on the account, Doritos had been pushing the nutritional aspect of their product, because their advertising was aimed squarely at moms. They wanted them to think of Doritos as a "good snack food." But teenagers were the ones doing all the eating, and the company was not connecting with them at all. Turns out moms and kids want different things from the foods they buy and eat. What worked with moms was not working with kids.

What did kids want from Doritos? The focus groups provided an interesting answer. At first, we were hearing what we expected to hear. Then one afternoon the moderator asked, "When do you eat them?"

"I eat a bag before a test," one kid said. Another told us, "I eat a whole bag when I'm on the phone with my friends." Now, at the time, I smoked almost two packs of cigarettes a day. I had an oral fixation. The kids, I realized, ate Doritos at the same times and for the same reasons I smoked. I sent a note into the room: "Ask them, 'If you eat a big family-size bag at noon, have you had lunch?'"

The answer was simple: "No."

The implication of this tiny negative was huge: Kids didn't think of Doritos as food. The company was selling food to moms, but that's not what kids wanted at all.

Based on that insight, our idea was to have the Doritos spokesman, Jay Leno, stop selling food and use his talent for observational humor to talk with kids about their eating behavior and oral fixations: why they ate Doritos, how they ate them, when they ate them, and whom they ate them with. Everything about the commercials was about why, when, and how kids wanted Doritos.

The ads talked about eating a whole bag of Doritos while shopping, then paying for an empty bag. They showed what the Doritos crunch sounded like inside kids' heads. They talked about sticking your whole face in the bag and inhaling the things—and other stuff the kids could relate to.

But honesty about behavior, especially when it comes with a wink and a smile, won't work as the central theme of a campaign unless both sides involved are honest about everything. It has to be a two-way street: We know what you're doing, and you know what we're doing. Our new tagline said it all: "Crunch All You Want. We'll Make More." It acknowledged, "You're eating these things by the bagful," while admitting, "We're taking money to the bank in buckets."

The ads worked like gangbusters because Doritos stopped selling food to moms and started seducing kids with what they really wanted: a big, crunchy bag of oral entertainment.

When crafting your message, ask yourself if you're merely selling your product's features instead of seducing your audience by talking about the benefits that interest them most.

Throwing Speedballs

How do you recognize a good idea? What is it that interrupts viewers' apathy, grabs their attention, and momentarily opens their minds to a new message?

In *Rhetoric,* a 2,500-year-old book on the art of persuasion, Aristotle describes a technique for engaging listeners called an enthymeme—literally meaning "something kept in mind." It's a way of using people's implicit assumptions to grab their attention. Here's the basic premise: If the first part of the speaker's statement confuses, the second part must explain. And if the first part explains, the second part should confuse. For example, Samuel Johnson could have said, "London has everything a man could possibly want to see or do." Instead he said, "When a man is tired of London, he is tired of life." The first part confuses and the second part explains. It's much more engaging.

Engagement is what it's all about. We are hardwired to respond to the discord caused by something that simultaneously confuses and informs. Our brain needs to take the next step to figure it out. And in order to do that, we need to get *involved.*

Advertisers have always recognized the persuasive power of enthymemes to draw an audience in:

With a name like Smucker's, it has to be good.

What happens in Vegas stays in Vegas.

Good times are waiting. Grab some Buds.

In space, no one can hear you scream.

Enthymemes work only when the person receiving the message understands what remains unstated. This is why the best advertising is actually "made" in the minds of the reader, listener, or viewer. And it involves a tantalizing cocktail of brain chemicals.

Great advertising gets into people's heads by combining adrenaline and dopamine. Adrenaline (also known as epinephrine) is a hormone and a neurotransmitter. It increases heart rate, constricts blood vessels, dilates air passages, and participates in the fight-or-flight response of the sympathetic nervous system. Dopamine plays a major role in the part of the brain that is responsible for reward-driven learning. Rewards increase the level of dopamine transmission in the brain, and a variety of several highly addictive drugs, including stimulants such as cocaine and methamphetamine, act directly on the mesolimbic dopamine system. How is that relevant to advertising? I'll show you.

Imagine what went through readers' heads in 1959 when they first saw the "Think Small" ad for the newly introduced Volkswagen Bug in *Life* magazine. *Whoa! What's this big empty white page of nothing?* The little VW Bug in the corner is not the main visual; the white space is. In a magazine packed wall-to-wall with photos, headlines, copy, and ads, a blank white page is confusing. It's weird. It doesn't make sense. Why all the white space? It was the visual equivalent of radio silence—making the reader think, "What the hell's going on? Is this a mistake? A misprint? I'm confused."

Think small.

Our little car isn't so much of a novelty any more.

A couple of dozen college kids don't try to squeeze inside it.

The guy at the gas station doesn't ask where the gas goes.

Nobody even stares at our shape.

In fact, some people who drive our little flivver don't even think 32 miles to the gallon is going any great guns.

Or using five pints of oil instead of five quarts.

Or never needing anti-freeze.

Or racking up 40,000 miles on a set of tires.

That's because once you get used to some of our economies, you don't even think about them any more.

Except when you squeeze into a small parking spot. Or renew your small insur-ance. Or pay a small repair bill. Or trade in your old VW for a new one.

Think it over.

Confusion grips you by getting your adrenaline going. Then the headline explains, "Think small." *Ah, it's not a big page of nothing. It's a picture of a small car. I get it. I figured it out. Thank you, brain. I'll take that shot of dopamine now.* It happens so quickly and subtly, you don't even realize it on a conscious level.

Disruption, confusion, agitation = adrenaline.

Explanation, comfort, confirmation = dopamine.

See? I've hooked you.

I like to think of modern conceptual advertising as throwing speedballs. A speedball is an injected mixture of heroin or another narcotic with cocaine or another stimulant. A strong advertising concept is like mixing together two drugs inside people's heads: a little hit of adrenaline and a little hit of dopamine in a fraction of a second. If the picture confuses, the headline explains. If the headline confuses, the picture explains.

It works the same way when a speaker opens a talk with a line that makes no sense until she explains it a few seconds later. Or when a thirty-second TV commercial opens with twenty-five seconds of footage that makes very little sense until an explanatory line of copy at the end rewards the viewer for hanging in there. This sense of confusion and explanation works in just about every medium. In fact, I'm just waiting for the day when web-page behavior becomes so expected and rote that online advertisers are willing to upend what people expect from the medium to make a point. What if after clicking on a Mr. Clean pop-up coupon and landing on Procter & Gamble's Mr. Clean website, everything—the words and pictures, logos and content—slid off the screen momentarily, leaving just a "super-clean" page. Maybe it's not a great idea, but it's an example of how in any medium the expected

> If the picture confuses, the headline explains. If the headline confuses, the picture explains.

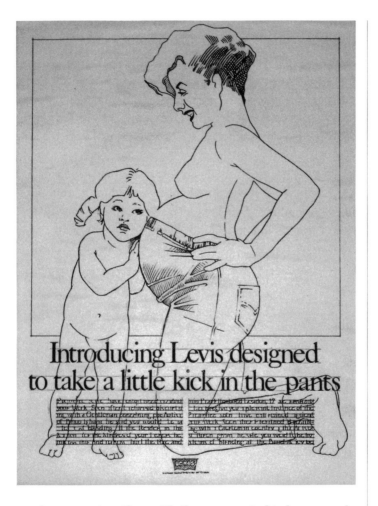

Introducing Levis designed
to take a little kick in the pants

can be woven together with the unexpected to keep people
engaged and the message interesting.

You don't learn about enthymemes in ad school.
Concept is the word modern communicators use to describe
an idea that engages. Even though an idea's inherent ability to engage is a basis of communication, most of us who
develop concepts for a living discover through trial and

error how to further engage the attention of others by using words and images, the expected and surprising, affinity and contrast.

I remember what it felt like the first time I created an ad that simultaneously confused and explained. Twenty-five years ago, I was working on my junior portfolio, trying to develop a concept for an ad for maternity Levi's. I wrote a headline, "Introducing Levi's designed to take a little kick in the pants." It made no sense at all without a visual to explain it—but combined with the right visual? Boom!

One moment I had no idea what an ad concept was, and the next moment I did. I felt it. I got it. And I was hooked.

Brands Aren't Magic— They're Math

I was working in the San Francisco office of a worldwide agency when one day the 150 offices around the globe simultaneously assembled their respective creative, account, and media people. The agency's main office, in New York, had completed a three-year initiative defining the company's position on branding. The document was being distributed to the agency's employees and its clients around the world. They gathered us all in the office's main entrance for the big unveiling.

I was in the back listening as the president of our office, the man tasked with making the presentation, held up an eight-hundred-page document. It was as thick as a phone book. Nobody was ever going to read it. Worse, by making it so dense, the agency was effectively admitting that it never intended anyone to read it. After all, these people knew to the letter exactly how much ad copy a reader of *Fortune* or the *Wall Street Journal* would read about high-tech products and software before losing interest and turning the page.

The agency president made it easier for us by telling us that the document explained the company's thinking about the relationship between the brand and the client's business. He held the document above his head and proclaimed it the agency's "Brand Bible," which made sense to me because a lot of what it said sounded very religious. The section on why a brand needed more than one defining attribute read, "A brand needs three defining attributes because four are too many and two are not enough." Oddly enough, that's the same reason you need to throw three wild pigs into a volcano to satisfy Pele, the Hawaiian goddess of fire and destruction.

It seemed to me that the idea of using advertising to build the brand, as opposed to using the brand to build the business, was leading me, the agency I worked for, and the whole advertising industry down a giant rabbit hole.

Companies are not brands. Logos are not brands. Products and services are not brands. Paris Hilton is not a brand.

A *brand* is just another word for a reputation that can be ruined by more than one person.

Back in the day, real live people stood behind their products. The names of Henry Ford, John D. Rockefeller, and Anita Roddick were synonymous with Ford Motor Company, Standard Oil, and the Body Shop. Over time, however, businesses grew from enterprises run by sole proprietors to much larger endeavors. As a result, they needed something other than one person to stand for all of the people who worked collectively to create their products. That's the role of a brand.

Today brands, not individuals, represent the reputations of businesses. A brand is the collective reputation made by a group of people united by a single, strategic purpose: making customers happy. The reputation of the entire company is affected if anyone in the group screws up.

Paris Hilton is not a brand because Paris Hilton's reputation can be ruined only by Paris Hilton. Only Paris Hilton makes the promise of what people can expect from her. Only she delivers on that promise. Therefore, Paris Hilton is the only one who can earn a reputation that only she can tarnish.

By contrast, for over fifty years, thousands of men and woman working at McCann-Erickson advertising agency offices around the globe told millions of people in different countries and in different languages what to expect from a Coca-Cola. And thousands of Coca-Cola workers, bottlers, truck drivers, and retail sales people made good on those promises with millions of cans and bottles of Coke. Any one of them could have screwed up and ruined or at least soiled the reputation of the Coca-Cola Company.

Building a real brand is the long, slow, back-and-forth process of using advertising to set the market's expectations, then delivering products that meet or exceed them. It's not a solo act. Brands are built together by ad agencies or other companies who make promises and by companies that make or provide products and services. Neither the promise-making company nor the product- or service-providing company is solely responsible for the brand. It's a two-way street.

The company offering the product or service is the one that foots the bill. It manages the brand—it pays advertising agencies, media companies, branding firms, and others

> A *brand* is just another word for a reputation that can be ruined by more than one person.

to set expectations in the market for its products and services. But nobody actually possesses the brand. Like a reputation, a brand can be built, managed, enhanced, guarded, and ruined. And also like a reputation, a brand is a perception that exists only in the minds and memories of those who have both expectations of the brand's promise and experience as to how the brand delivers on its promise. In other words, the thing brand-building companies buy and pay for exists only in people's heads.

I've heard that the Coca-Cola Company keeps the recipe for Coke in a vault below its Atlanta headquarters. The brand the company has spent a gazillion dollars building, however, is kept in the minds of its customers. The Coke logo is all over Atlanta. Yet the Coke *brand* is invisible, ephemeral. It's by far the most valuable thing the company has built, but it's nowhere to be found in the building.

Reputations are built one successfully fulfilled promise at a time.

Traditional brand building is the process of taking a new product or service that nobody knows or cares about and—using words, pictures, music, and stories—creating a promise so compelling to a group of people that, when those products and services make good on that promise, a reputation is rooted so strongly in those consumers' minds that they cannot imagine their life without that product.

Apple promises to eliminate complexity and ugliness from people's lives. Facebook promises to give people the power to share and make the world more open and connected. Michelin promises safe travels. Products and services are the *way* a company delivers on its promise; the brand is the reputation the company earns for how *well* it delivers.

Reputations
are built one
successfully
fulfilled
promise at
a time.

When people talk about a brand as if it's an advertising agency's responsibility or invention, I don't know what to do. When I think of a brand as a reputation-building process, however, I know exactly what to do, because I understand the equation: Promise + successful delivery = good reputation.

Warren Buffett once said, "It takes twenty years to build a reputation and five minutes to ruin it. If you think about that, you'll do things differently."

I would add that it can take thousands of people to establish and maintain a worldwide reputation but only one or a few to ruin it. If you think about that, you'll do things differently too. A company can have thousands of well-trained, helpful employees, but if one YouTube video of a surly sixteen-year-old employee goes viral, the reputation of the business takes a real hit.

Recently I saw that an employee at a national upscale, indie-and-earthy woman's retail clothing chain asked a customer who was breast-feeding her baby in the store to do so in the store's bathroom. Inside of twenty-four hours, the insulted customer invited her other breast-feeding friends to join her in a protest at the store. Before long, the store was issuing apologies on national TV. The actions of one employee had become a full-blown branding disaster.

A brand's usefulness as a concept is in direct proportion to the number of people working on the business who can ruin it. Seven hundred thousand people work for Coca-Cola, so it's probably smart for company leaders to think about protecting—as well as growing—the brand. Keeping employees happy, informed, and involved is an excellent way to do this.

For small companies, startups, or individuals, however, it's better to concentrate on building a reputation.

Products and services are the *way* a company delivers on its promise; the brand is the reputation the company earns for how *well* it delivers.

Promise +
successful
delivery =
good
reputation.

As long as you can fit everyone responsible for the success or failure of your business into one room, there's no need to use the word *brand*. It's too abstract and tends to sound like a stand-alone entity that can be built or addressed in and of itself. Try using the word *reputation* instead. It's much more compelling and causes people to care a little more.

One Question,
Four Answers

By the time I'd been in advertising for ten years,
I'd heard clients ask some odd questions. Once,
after presenting a client with an idea for a TV
commercial and deflecting a series of what-ifs like
"What if people don't like dogs?" and "What if
they don't know what guacamole is supposed to
look like?" the client asked the agency, "What if a
family doesn't have their TV on?"

Once, a client asked, "Is there a rule of thumb for the
ratio of 'brand' to 'sell' in a commercial?" I didn't know
how to begin to think about that one, but I couldn't let it
go. Eventually that question changed the way I thought
about advertising.

Until hearing that question, I had believed that the
agency-client relationship was symbiotic and simple.
On one side were the concerns of the agency's creatives:
doing everything possible to make the product emotionally
appealing and human. On the other side were the client's
rational concerns: making sure the factual, quantifiable

claims about their products or services came across loud and clear.

I felt that the clients and the creatives were locked in a constant battle for the soul of the brand. Either the brand could be likable, relatable, and beloved; or it could be informational, reliable, and pragmatic. In this worldview, these were two mutually exclusive goals. In my mind, the answer to how much brand (emotion) and how much sell (fact) was an either-or choice. Augmenting one diminished the other. But that belief began to change the more I reflected on this question.

I began to sort through all the briefs I could find for every print ad, poster, radio spot, and television commercial I had worked on up to that point. I was looking to see what they had in common when it came to mandatory facts, support points, and the emotional takeaway.

I found that—regardless of the medium—every bit of advertising I had ever worked on was essentially trying to do one of four things:

- Introduce a new product or service.
- Incite trial through limited-time offers, such as sales or events.
- Inspire loyalty by reminding consumers of a unique or differentiating benefit of a product or service.
- Identify with consumers by demonstrating shared values or attitudes.

Until then, I'd thought building a brand required choosing between being emotional and evoking feelings or being rational and transferring facts. Gradually I realized that the process involved doing *both*. The question was when and how to use facts and feelings. I divided the four types of ads into the following categories: introductory, trial, differentiating, and mutual-love-and-respect. Each of these provokes a particular emotional response and takeaway in the minds of consumers.

Introductory ads are designed to inspire curiosity. They usually herald big news or include information about some form of added product utility. Consider the teaser campaign for HBO's original series *True Blood*. It featured outdoor posters advertising a new drink called TruBlood (available at trubeverage.com) and posters in major markets promoting equal rights for vampires. Neither poster series mentioned the TV show, but both had an emotional appeal that made people very curious.

Trial ads create a sense of urgency. Often these ads include a limited-time offer (LTO) to signal that something about the business proposition is temporary. Think Labor Day Sale or Mother's Day Sale or "available only while supplies last." In LTOs, the facts are critical. "This offer ends tomorrow!" "Tickets go on sale Friday." You need to mention these facts in order to create urgency.

Differentiating ads build on the brand relationship. They increase market share by reminding people about the unique difference that sets a product or service apart from everyone else's in the category. Think about taglines like Federal Express's "When it absolutely, positively has to get there overnight"; Bounty, "the quicker picker-upper"; or Taco Bell's "Think outside the bun."

Mutual-love-and-respect ads keep customers by making them part of an exclusive club. These ads are all about protecting your margins by appealing to the loyal audience that matters to you most. Examples include "insider"-type advertising that speaks to a very specific and exclusive audience, such as Apple's "Think different" campaign.

I also noticed that these four kinds of ads provided a natural progression. I stopped looking at the branding process as an either-or proposition. It wasn't about appealing either to the head with rational facts, figures, and economic benefits *or* to the heart by evoking emotions to make the brand friendly, trusted, *or* aspirational. Instead, I started to see persuasion as a here-to-there kind of thing. Start with a product or service nobody knows. Use the appropriate combination of words, pictures, music, and stories to transfer facts *and* evoke emotions. Using the four types of ads over time, turn that product or service into something that someone somewhere can't imagine living without.

With my four different kinds of ads, I considered my client's original question. Is there a proper ratio of facts to emotions present in every persuasive message?

- In **introductory** and **mutual-love-and-respect ads,** emotional appeal powers the message.
- **Trial ads** are driven by a fact-based limited-time offer.
- The **differentiating ads** look like a fifty-fifty split. Yes, there is an optimal ratio, but it varies according to the type of ad.

Because of one odd question, I stopped looking at the agency-client relationship as a constant struggle between hard facts and emotional appeals. Now, I saw it as a pas de deux; sometimes emotions lead the way and sometimes facts move the process along. Building a brand isn't about either transferring facts or evoking emotions. It's about using facts and emotions in different ways to achieve different results.

Dissecting a Frog
Is Easy; Making O
Is Hard

When I first got into the advertising business,
I would often get stuck, go blank, and experience
an art director's equivalent of writer's block when
trying to come up with ideas. So I did what stuck
people do. I picked up books written by experts
describing their advertising beliefs and methods.
I'd thumb through awards annuals hoping to find
something I could use to solve my problem without
actually copying someone else's great ad.

There was just one hitch to this approach. Reading
about other people's experience and looking at other
people's ads did not actually help me come up with ideas.
In fact, reading successful stories about how other people
came up with really good ideas usually made me feel envi-
ous or stupid or both. What's more, trying to separate the

a
em
quires
a weird
combination
of freedom
and
constraint.

principle that makes an ad good from the actual execution of the ad itself is an exercise in academic wheel spinning that just made me and everyone around me feel anxious and angry, especially when we were working under a tight deadline.

Although analyzing what's been done by others can be somewhat informative, one of the things I really like about advertising agencies is that they are practical places where things need to get done, presented, sold, written, bid, produced, and sent out the door *today*. Agencies are not big on criticism, deconstruction, and analysis of work that has nothing to do with the job at hand. Agencies exist in the here, now, and near future. There is talk about what the competition is *doing* but not a lot of history or theory.

When I was stuck with a problem, history wasn't that helpful anyway. I would usually resort to looking at what I had to do and what my parameters were. Time after time, I realized that one thing was true: Solving a problem requires a weird combination of freedom and constraint.

Whenever I hear "Just have fun with it" or "Think outside the box," I know from experience that things are about to turn into a colossal waste of time. One of the biggest misconceptions about developing advertising is that freedom improves creativity. In my experience, it's just the opposite. Give smart, ambitious, creative people a tight brief, a list of mandatory elements, and seemingly no way to make a project interesting, and they will figure out how to claw their way out of the box and prove that the tight brief, requirements, and mandatories are nothing compared to the awesome power of imagination. Nevertheless, creative people need room to move *and* some sense that they are standing on terra firma and heading in the right direction.

Karate sensei have an expression that translates as "finger to the south." It means that when giving instruction in a practical art or craft, a teacher can point the way, but it is the students who must learn by doing and take the journey themselves.

Based on my own advertising experience and inspired by one client's question about the ideal relationship of facts to feelings in ads (explained in "One Question, Four Answers"), I put together a model or guide that helped me see *what to do* to solve about 95 percent of the tactical problems I confronted. Unlike a how-to formula (which most creatives are suspicious of anyway), my model was more like a road map that showed me where the ideas I needed could most likely be found. Over the years, I refined it and used it to create ad campaigns, win business, and succeed at seducing strangers. It's outlined in the next section.

Now, finger to the south.

Part Two
Four Secret Ways
Out of the Box

"When you frame a sentence, shoot with a single bullet and hit that one thing alone."

—Woodrow Wilson's father to his son, when teaching him to read and write

The Four Fundamental Questions

Every message that is trying to persuade, sell, or seduce needs to answer one of the four fundamental questions people ask before choosing any product or service:

- What is it?
- Why do I need it now?
- What makes it different from other things?
- Who else thinks it's good?

Answering these questions intriguingly, economically, truthfully, and memorably is the art of advertising.

The conundrum of advertising is that for a message to break through to, connect with, and motivate a prospect, it can answer only one of these questions at a time. It takes a very different kind of message to answer each question.

FACTS, FEELIN
BUSINESS GOALS

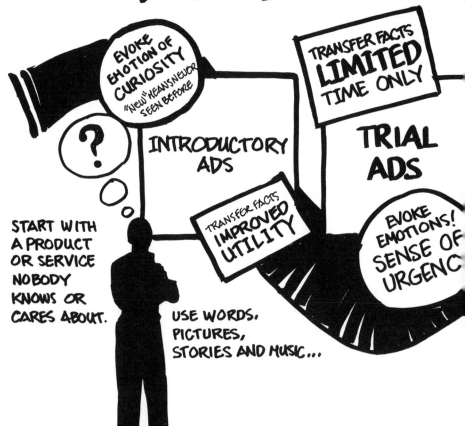

EVOKE EMOTION OF CURIOSITY
"NEW" MEANS NEVER SEEN BEFORE

TRANSFER FACTS
LIMITED TIME ONLY

?

INTRODUCTORY ADS

TRIAL ADS

TRANSFER FACTS
IMPROVED UTILITY

EVOKE EMOTIONS!
SENSE OF URGENC

START WITH A PRODUCT OR SERVICE NOBODY KNOWS OR CARES ABOUT.

USE WORDS, PICTURES, STORIES AND MUSIC...

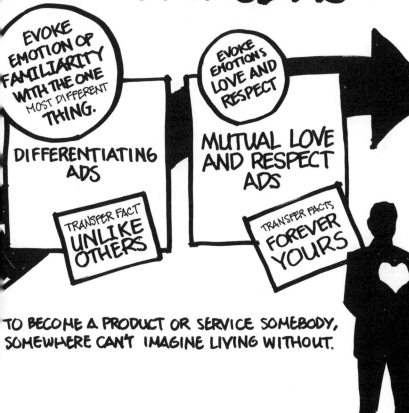

AND THE FOUR
OF ADVERTISERS

EVOKE EMOTION OF FAMILIARITY WITH THE ONE MOST DIFFERENT THING.

DIFFERENTIATING ADS

TRANSFER FACT **UNLIKE OTHERS**

EVOKE EMOTIONS LOVE AND RESPECT

MUTUAL LOVE AND RESPECT ADS

TRANSFER FACTS **FOREVER YOURS**

TO BECOME A PRODUCT OR SERVICE SOMEBODY, SOMEWHERE CAN'T IMAGINE LIVING WITHOUT.

As I mentioned earlier, throughout my first ten years in advertising, I had been asked to create only four different types of messages. Each message is tied to a specific goal.

Introductory ads are used to deliver a fresh announcement to an audience—for example, about a brand-new or recently improved product. Trial ads are designed to inspire the test of a product or service and include a sense of urgency that makes the audience eager to act *now*. Differentiating ads define what's unique to a product or why it's right for a particular user. Shared-values ads— or what I call mutual-love-and-respect ads—are about a company's *customers* and relate so intimately to them that they often resemble short stories, little teleplays, or inside jokes that make sense only to that group.

Seeing how each of these four kinds of advertising messages related to each other in a linear progression made me rethink how advertising worked, how I did my job, and how I went about looking for solutions to communication problems.

The illustration on the previous pages is read left to right, horizontally. You can see that a brand-building campaign begins with the introduction of a product or service no one knows about and uses these four kinds of ads to build a relationship over time between customers and the company, based on shared values and aspirations.

What Is It?
Introductory Ads

What is this thing? What's it doing? What are you talking about? What's it to me?

The goal of an introductory ad is to increase inquiries, and the best way to do that is by arousing curiosity. Look at the two words most commonly used in product introductions: *new* and *improved.* "New" says you've never seen this before. "Improved" indicates added utility. Both make people curious.

As noted previously in the section about enthymemes, people are made curious when presented with an ambiguous, unresolved, or incomplete message. The best way to arouse curiosity and generate inquiries is by leaving something out.

I'm constantly attracted to ads that omit something important. A short teaser usually works best on me: the five foods designed to eliminate belly fat or three stocks you must buy this year. I need to know what's on the list.

In ads in traditional media, like newspapers, the headline's job is to hook people and make them curious enough to read the copy. Today a banner or pop-up might do the job of raising a question like "Is your tap water safe?" or "Will you have enough money to retire?" Regardless of medium,

> The best way to arouse curiosity and generate inquiries is by leaving something out.

the point of introductory ads is to generate inquiries by creating a message, headline, banner, post, or tweet that makes people curious.

An introductory ad's success can be measured any number of ways, from store visits and incoming phone calls to webpage hits and click-throughs—in short, anything that tells you that your message made people curious enough to want to know more.

WHAT IS IT?

THE GOAL OF INTRODUCTORY ADS IS TO INCREASE INQUIRIES.

The Curious Case of Soviet Jeans

A sportswear campaign I did for Seattle Pacific Industries (SPI) was my first experiment in developing introductory commercials that deliberately left out a critical piece of the puzzle. It was the first time I worked on a product introduction that was so tied to a particular moment that I knew our messaging, the target audience, and media strategy all needed to align to make someone someplace really curious— or the client would be screwed.

It was January 1990, and the company had just acquired the brand Soviet Jeans—casual menswear with an industrial, behind-the-Iron-Curtain look. SPI wanted our agency to create an ad campaign that would make the brand look big enough and cool enough to attract the attention of clothing buyers at an upcoming trade show in Las Vegas. At the time, Levi's and Calvin Klein were spending many millions of dollars apiece on marketing. We had one million.

The agency decided to take advantage of the sudden interest in Soviet paraphernalia that had come about after the fall of the Berlin Wall the previous October. Even though the wall had come down, both sides were still suspicious of each other. But even if we weren't exactly friendly yet, it appeared that, for the first time in years, we were no longer determined to blow each other up.

We capitalized on this uneasy détente by creating a campaign that showed American men engaged in American conflicts but wearing Soviet Jeans. In every spot, just as things looked as though they were about to get violent, someone said something in Russian, and the situation was defused. The end frame read, "Soviet Jeans. Work it out." In two of the spots, we cast actual gang members, who generated their own storm of publicity. Black gang members speaking Russian? There were no subtitles. The ads were surreal.

We ran the commercials on the Grammy Awards broadcast in Los Angeles, Chicago, and New York—where most of the country's retail buyers live and work. The ads also ran on the closed-circuit TV network in Las Vegas hotel rooms—so the convention attendees who worked in retail wouldn't miss them. It seemed the Soviet Jeans campaign was everywhere.

The campaign generated free press and publicity worth ten times our budget. The commercials weren't an announcement; they were a riddle. Nobody knew whether to be impressed, upset, offended, or—as in the case of the buyers—anxious enough to just buy the damn things and see what happened.

The introductory advertising did its job—Soviet Jeans were on department-store shelves and not in the SPI warehouses.

Why Do I Need It Now? Limited-Time Offers

Hurry! Soak up all the career-saving marketing tips you can. Because this chapter is disappearing in five . . . four . . . three . . .

Feel the urgency?

That's the beauty of a limited-time offer (LTO). These ads are designed to temporarily bump traffic, trials, or sales. The best ones do this by instilling a sense of urgency with phrases such as "this weekend only," "available only while supplies last," "opening this Friday at a theater near you," or, in the case of the Home Shopping Network, "only five left."

The media strategy to use when trying to boost sales is frequent and local. Radio and local newspaper advertising is still dominated by these messages. And the metric for success is, unsurprisingly, increased sales, trials, and traffic.

LTOs are mostly fact-based messages that are aimed at market shoppers—people who have already made inquiries and are interested in buying. The catch—and opportunity—is that market shoppers are usually waiting for the best opportunity or price before they pull the trigger.

LTOs are designed to temporarily bump traffic, trials, or sales.

Market shoppers can be really dangerous to a business. Unlike a company's most profitable customers—the 20 percent who typically account for 80 percent of the business—market shoppers are the 80 percent of customers who account for only 20 percent of the business. The problem is there are so many of them that a business can get duped into thinking that it depends on them. Pretty soon the business cuts back on service, selection, quality, and all the good things that attract profitable high-end customers. Instead, the business is left with customers who buy a lot of cheap stuff that doesn't bring in much money. When a company starts spending a large part of its marketing budget to attract customers who account for so little profit, its days are numbered.

Another danger of LTOs is that companies get hooked on the bump and want to run them all the time. As a result, their limited-time offers are no longer limited, and the sensation of urgency dulls in the public's perception. You've seen shops with the permanent 75% OFF sign in the window. Does the sign entice you to go in there?

Limited-time offers as a communication strategy are like getting a business hooked on drugs. It takes more and more marketing dollars to get fewer and fewer people excited about bigger and bigger discounts.

Why buy now when X Company will be having another sale next week? J.C. Penney showed us a good example of what happens when a company quits an addiction to LTOs cold turkey. In the fall of 2011, after a fifteen-year strategy of running one sale after another, retailer J.C. Penney brought in CEO Ron Johnson to turn the place around. Johnson stopped the sales, and it did not go well. An article in *Forbes* magazine summed up how it went down:

"Johnson aims to steer J.C. Penney away from the high-promotional activity common among department stores. He has already tweaked J.C. Penney's sales strategy, assuming an everyday-low-price approach. Yet, that confused many of J.C. Penney's customers—shoppers accustomed to coupons and frequent promotions. Johnson admitted he misjudged how customers would react to the change. 'We failed at that,' he says."

As strange as it seems, the best way to get people to try, sample, or buy is to somehow limit their ability to do so.

WHY DO I NEED IT NOW?

THE GOAL OF LIMITED TIME OFFERS IS TO BUMP SALES OR TRAFFIC.

J.C. Penney's customers left in droves. Just seventeen months after he was hired, Johnson was gone, too. He failed to anticipate what to do after what the company was currently doing stopped working—not to mention misunderstanding his audience's expectations.

As strange as it seems, the best way to get people to try, sample, or buy is to somehow limit their ability to do so. Urgency is also created when people feel they need to act before an opportunity gets away. A good price is important, but it's even more effective when it's on the other side of a window of opportunity that will close soon.

The only time I run around my house in a frenzy is when I've chosen seats from an online theater reservation system. I've clicked the button and suddenly a clock pops up, letting me know that I have only three minutes to enter my credit-card number before my seats disappear. The next two minutes of my life are spent running around the house looking for my credit card while my wife counts down the remaining time in ten-second increments. Seeing my previously available seats turn from pleasant green to sold-out red right before my eyes creates, at least in my experience, a terrifying sense of urgency.

Soon we'll see smart online marketers showing stock dwindling from their shelves. Car dealers will show cars disappearing from their lots. Clothing retailers will show clothes vanishing from their racks. And hotels will show rooms filling up before online shoppers' eyes.

Craigslist, eBay, and specialized sites like AutoTrader have almost replaced local classified advertising. However, as local marketers and stores become more sophisticated with their online efforts, you'll start noticing something new when you search or shop for something online. Instead of pop-ups and banner ads from well-known stores like

Amazon and Zappos, you'll soon see banners and pop-ups from *local* stores, letting you know that they still have one or two of the items you want close by and in stock. To compete with large, national low-price players, local marketers will need to step up the urgency by creating very small, personal-size windows through which people can see very big opportunities disappear really fast.

The next generation of online advertising will be less about companies letting you know what's on sale and more about making you aware of opportunity slipping away. Your competitors may be planning it already. The clock is ticking.

What Makes It Different? Differentiating Ads.

Differentiating is where great reputations are made and great brands are built. This is where advertising's long-term benefits lie, because differentiating is about making a promise to the market that is unique, relevant, and memorable. This is where company taglines that have run for years or even decades are born. And it's the one place where business, culture, poetry, Darwinism, battle, and beauty all collide.

A side from procreating and dying, differentiating is what we're here to do.

The best differentiating campaigns may cement a company's reputation and make a product's unique benefit so much a part of the culture that it forever alters the market. The BMW ad campaign does a beautiful job of highlighting the status and distinction that their product confers. Why drive any other vehicle if you have both the means to own and the ability to recognize "The Ultimate Driving Machine"?

The job of a differentiating campaign is to find new ways to illustrate your brand promise and keep it relevant to potential new customers. When working in this area, the challenge is to find another way or another medium or another story that makes a product or company's promise even truer than it was before.

I love ad campaigns like the one L.A. Eyeworks ran for more than a decade. The store sells eyeglass frames and made a name for itself with a series of ads featuring beautiful black-and-white portraits of celebrities like artist Andy Warhol and actor Arnold Schwarzenegger wearing L.A. Eyeworks glasses. The headline read, "A face is like a work of art. It deserves a great frame." The thing I loved about the campaign was that every additional new face made the statement more true. Blackglama did the same sort of thing for their furs. Their stunning print ads each featured one famous woman—a designer, singer, or actress—wearing a Blackglama fur. The headline on all of them read, "What becomes a Legend most?" The Absolut Vodka campaign that featured the bottle as a part of the landscape was another memorable example. And so is the famous "Got milk?" campaign. Every new ad or illustration makes the one differentiating statement or promise more true.

> A tagline is a declaration of a company's promise to the market.

What Makes Differentiating Different

Taglines are one of the most effective ways to easily establish what's different about your product or service. A tagline is a declaration of a company's promise to the market. It's like a raison d'être in seven words or less.

We bring good things to life.

You're in good hands with Allstate.

Finger-lickin' good.

Think different.

Tastes great. Less filling.

A diamond is forever.

Drivers wanted.

According to Dan Wieden of Nike's longtime ad agency Wieden+Kennedy, presenting a new tagline is like selling a client an empty bucket. Every ad that's signed with that tagline fills the bucket a little more with each new exposure. It can take years to fill that thing—and solidify your reputation.

Once a company discovers a differentiating promise that is unique, memorable, and relevant, it needs to live with it. It is both a public declaration, "This is what I am," and a public commitment, "This is what I'm here to do for you." It embodies perfectly the principle of zeroing in on and choosing a single business goal.

Smart companies will change or update or add to their product line to make good on their promise over time. That's what keeps the customer relationship fresh and vital. For instance, if Pepsi's promise is to be "The Taste of a New Generation," its products need to reflect that. If the tastes of the new generation change, so should Pepsi's products. The promise, however, can stay right where it is.

Zig When Others Zag

Another strategic way to set yourself apart is by being contrary and doing the opposite of what people expect.

Jordin Mendelsohn of Mendelsohn/Zien Advertising was by far the sharpest, bravest, and most unflinching strategic message maker or advertising creative I've ever worked with. He had a sixth sense for making the biggest, once-in-a-blue-moon, strategic messages out of the smallest, everyday, tactical opportunities.

WHAT MAKES IT DIFFERENT FROM OTHER THINGS?

THE GOAL OF DIFFERENTIATING ADS IS TO INCREASE MARKET SHARE.

Once, a car company Jordin was working for won a Car of the Year award. Instead of recommending that the client run an ad congratulating itself, Jordin disappeared into his office and came out an hour later with a number of arguments as to why it would do the client more good to refuse the award than accept it. First of all, the other cars nominated were trash, not even in the same league. It would diminish the client's car even to compete with them. Second, it was a minor award, not the Motor Trend Car of the Year award. Jordin figured it was better to keep pushing the company's engineers to win the real award than to run around collecting tin trophies. Third, there would be free publicity in refusing the award. Jordin eventually convinced the client to run an ad refusing the award, giving the reason that the other cars in the competition were so inferior that accepting the award would do the company's reputation more harm than good.

This was a great example of what marketing gurus Al Ries and Jack Trout called the law of category in their book *The 22 Immutable Laws of Marketing*. If you can't be first in a category, set up a new category you can own. Instead of being another car to win the award, be the first car to turn it down. Rather than running a forgettable self-congratulatory ad about winning the award, Jordin opted to make a stink, throw a fit, define his own high ground, rise above the award, and differentiate his car client from every other Car of the Year recipient forever.

Differentiating ads boost market share by creating a sense of affinity between consumers and the one essential difference that sets a product apart from its competitors in a category: the unique selling proposition, sometimes referred to as the USP. Differentiating ads are the engine that can change a little-known product or service with a difference into the number-one brand in a market.

The target audience for these messages are a business's "market makers"—the people for whom a good match between what they want and what you've got is more important than a good price. They are in the market for that difference, and they are willing to pay for it. So show it clearly. Say it loud. Make choosing what they want to choose easy for them.

That Old Familiar Feeling

Everything about a differentiating campaign is designed to make the target customer feel familiar with and loyal to a company's promise and products. One highly effective way to do this is through a corporate sponsorship, such as appearing regularly at certain places or times in order to become a familiar part of the goings-on. Television programs, sporting events, podcasts, websites, magazines, and concerts are terrific ways to bond with your audience by going where they go and doing what they do.

Measuring Success

Because the stakes are so high and access to competitors' sales data is limited, it's hard to know exactly how well differentiating campaigns are working or whether or not a company's market share is growing. Companies pay big research companies big money to watch and track how advertising spending affects the sales of products and services in a category. On the fly, unit-sales mix is often a good metric of a differentiating campaign's success. For example, if a company sees growth in its premium line—the products that best express the purest form of their unique selling proposition—you can usually bet that the attempt at differentiation has been effective.

Here's a more specific example: If BMW is differentiating itself from other cars by advertising that it's "The Ultimate Driving Machine," and the BMW M3 is the ultimate BMW, the advertising has likely been successful at building market share if sales of that model go up more than sales of other BMWs.

A Shade Different— Belle Jolie

In the first season of *Mad Men,* Matt Weiner had decided that he wanted to follow the journey of the character of Peggy Olson from being just another girl in Sterling Cooper's secretarial pool to becoming a young copywriter finding her identity and voice in the man's world of Madison Avenue circa 1960.

In order to differentiate Peggy from the other women in the office, we created a story about her differentiating one lipstick company from the others. The client, Belle Jolie, was known for offering a large selection of colors. To see which shades of lipstick women found most attractive, Sterling Cooper staged a focus group made up of the agency's secretarial pool.

In the following scene between Peggy and Freddie Rumson, an old-school copywriter, we see how Peggy distinguishes herself from the other girls by her creative way of seeing things. In the process, she also reveals her instincts for differentiating products. The tissues Peggy collects in this scene are covered with the blotted lip prints of the focus group participants.

Mark Your Man

FIRE ROSE RED

Lorem ipsum dolor sit amet, consectetuer adipiscing elit, sed diam nonummy nibh euismod tincidunt ut laoreet dolore magna aliquam erat volutpat. Ut wisi enim ad minim veniam, quis nostrud exerci tation ullamcorper suscipit lobortis nisl ut aliquip ex ea commodo

Belle Jolie

Episode 105, "Babylon," as broadcast, draft, written by André Jacquemetton, Maria Jacquemetton, and Matthew Weiner

INTERIOR, STERLING COOPER RESEARCH ROOM (Day 3)

The room is now in complete DISARRAY. Lipsticks and tissues all over the place. Peggy helps Joan with the cleaning up. Fred comes in.

                    FRED
     Now we have to count the shades they tried. Could
     you bring me those tissues, dear?

Peggy hands him the wastebasket filled with tissues.

                    PEGGY
     Here's your basket of kisses.

                    FRED
     Basket of kisses. That's cute. Who told you that?

                    PEGGY
     What do you mean?

                    FRED
     Where did you hear that?

                    PEGGY
     I just thought of it. Isn't that what it is?

Fred keys in on her.

                    FRED
     It is, sweetheart. (beat) Which color did you
     like?

                    PEGGY
     I didn't get the one I liked. Someone took my
     color.

                    FRED
     Why didn't you choose another one?

                    PEGGY
     I'm very particular.

                    FRED
     As opposed to the other girls.

                    PEGGY
     I don't know. I don't think anybody wants to be
     one of a hundred colors in a box.

For Peggy, a wide range of colors was not important. The benefit was about finding *her* color, a personal signifier. Discovering the differentiating color was what was most important to women.

Each of the three ads that Peggy developed for Belle Jolie lipsticks features a single woman with a single lipstick. Instead of the company's old ads that showed hundreds of lipsticks and a range of colors, the new one showed one woman with one lipstick and one man in the background with a big kiss on the side of his face. The headline on all three ads reads: "Mark Your Man."

It falls to Don to explain the difference between marketing and selling to the Belle Jolie executives who think they want the range of colors to be the focal point of the campaign. Don says, "Every woman wants choices, but in the end, none wants to be one in a box of a hundred. You are giving every girl who wears your lipstick the gift of total ownership."

Peggy's emotionally powerful insight is the first time we realize that she is a creature unlike any other and that Peggy Olson, like all of the best differentiators, will make her distinctive mark in the world.

Those of us working in the real world of persuasion can help our clients make their marks by reminding them of the empowering value of differentiating ads. When done well, these messages help consumers make the right choice for themselves by clearly pointing out the differences between one product and another, making it easy for people to choose the product or service or company that is most right for them.

Who Else Thinks It's Good? Mutual-Love-and-Respect Ads

Mutual-love-and-respect ads, or shared-values ads, are about the unique traits, backgrounds, styles, behaviors, habits, and tastes that make one company's *customers* different from all others, as opposed to differentiating ads, which are about how one company's *products* are different. I think of them as thank-you notes or inside jokes.

These customers are the ones who matter most to a company's profits or margins, because they buy more than the company's products and services. They buy into the company as a whole—its idea, philosophy, point of view, values, promise, and purpose. These people are family. They identify with the company, and their identity depends on the company. Often these are the people the product, service, or company were made for.

Bikers are a good example. Bikers need Harley-Davidson in order to be bikers, and Harley-Davidson needs bikers in order to be Harley-Davidson. The company once celebrated its unique audience with a series of Harley-Davidson clothing ads that featured beautiful black-and-white photos of bikers. They made these guys with their greasy jeans, long beards, wraparound shades, and Harley-Davidson leathers look like iron icons. Personal acknowledgment like this reinforces the loyalty of customers who so identify with a product that they will buy it at a premium.

These ads are not about selling or seducing. Mutual-love-and-respect ads are about *cementing*. In fact, these messages are like dog whistles. The whole point is that only certain people can hear them.

Because the product, service, or company often originated for—or emerged from—this select group, these messages are also like love letters or inside jokes. The only important fact transferred is the identity of the sender, which is usually the company name or logo. The emotion these messages are designed to evoke is the security of knowing that a soul mate exists who understands me, the customer, wholeheartedly. These ads feature images or stories about shared secrecy, conspiracy, or insider acknowledgments.

Nike once developed a "Runners Are Different" ad campaign that celebrated runners. It worked brilliantly because it spoke to their core customer who was, first and foremost, a runner. Not an athlete, not a cross-trainer, not a basketball player—a runner. One ad in the campaign showed a bare-chested marathoner putting Band-Aids over his nipples before a race. What? Marathoners know that after twenty-six miles of running, a nylon or cotton

T-shirt can feel like sandpaper to a nipple. I'm not a runner. I didn't know that. I remember looking at the ad for ten minutes trying to figure out what it was talking about. Then it occurred to me that the person the ad was talking to was most definitely not me.

In the last few years, Ketel One Vodka has come up with my favorite mutual-love-and-respect ads. The ads from their "Dear Ketel One Drinker" campaign illustrate how this kind of advertising answers the question, "Who else thinks it's good?"

WHO ELSE THINKS IT'S GOOD?

THE GOAL OF MUTUAL-LOVE-AND-RESPECT ADS **IS TO INCREASE** AND PROTECT MARGINS.

Sometimes it is *only* the users of a product or service that differentiate it from others. There is not much difference among vodkas, but only a small "batch" of drinkers drink Ketel One. By the same token, there is not a lot of difference between Coke and Pepsi or among the many brands of jeans or cotton T-shirts. Likewise, all football teams have fans, but only the Green Bay Packers have Cheeseheads. When advertising or promoting a product or service that is not much different from the competition, look at the people who use it. Ask what makes them different. Make note of where the product or service comes from and find out what makes that place different. Consider the reasons people identify with different countries, cities, neighborhoods, bands, clubs, schools, trades, looks, and lifestyles.

Mark Twain said, "It were not best that we should all think alike; it is difference of opinion that makes horse races." And sometimes a difference of opinion makes a really successful advertising campaign.

Dear Ketel One Drinker Thank you.

It's Not About Me—
It's About You

Here's an example of a successful ad designed to celebrate what makes a company's *customers* different from other people in the marketplace. It's a Kia Sportage ad developed specifically for Generation Y, aka millennials, born in the 1980s. Gen Y is the world's first digitally native generation of car buyers.

In 2001, while working at the ad agency David&Goliath, my creative partner, Kim Genkinger, and I were asked to reintroduce the Kia Sportage SUV to a new young audience. There were over 140 SUV makes and models on the road. The commercials for all of them looked pretty much the same. The car traveled from city to country. The close-up shot showed a big front tire splashing through mud or water and going over a log or boulder. The shot was always tilted, or "dutched," at a forty-five-degree angle so it looked even more energetic. All SUVs do everything. All of them go everywhere. All have all the features that let you do whatever you want to do.

Instead of the car, we thought about the young drivers. Kia makes great cars with great warranties, and they don't cost a lot. Because their customers tend to be young, a Kia is often their first new car. We asked the question: What made these young people, these Generation Y SUV drivers, different from other SUV drivers, like Baby Boomers or Generation X folks?

Baby Boomers, the generation that values authenticity above almost everything else, were the first to drive big, rugged sport-utility vehicles. Naturally they gravitated to brands like Jeep, an SUV with a war record, and Land Rover, an SUV built for the African savanna and the Australian outback.

The Nissan Xterra was built to be the SUV for Generation X, those fiercely independent latchkey kids born between 1960 and 1980 who reject rules and limits and dislike authority. Nissan designed a first-aid kit into the Xterra after discovering in focus groups that Gen X-ers consider their emotional and physical scars badges of honor and part of their adventure.

Generation Y kids are mellow, positive, and forward-looking people who share and network and make stuff happen together. They are the generation who went into their dorm rooms at night and, fueled by Red Bull and Gummy Bears, worked together to build and expand the biggest thing that mankind has ever made: the Internet. They tend to think that good things happen when everybody does their part. When everyone contributes what they can—edits a page, crowdsources, or donates their five dollars—cool things happen.

That's why we made a car ad for a generation who sees the world as flat and connected. The commercial was not about one person doing everything. It followed one car through one day as a bunch of young, optimistic people used it to do something good, then tossed the car's keys to someone else who used it to do their thing, and so on. The spot had a driving music track about living a good life and not taking anything for granted. It sounded and felt like an anthem. At the end of the spot was a line of copy that said, "The KIA Sportage. The SUV with everything is now for everyone."

There was not a lot in the commercial about what made the Kia Sportage different from the 140 other SUVs out there. The spot was a huge hit because it made the Kia Sportage look like the first SUV made expressly for the first generation of Internet-native drivers.

Kia ran focus groups after the spot ran. Young people who saw it said, "If I were there, I'd hope one of those people would throw me the keys." The commercial made members of Generation Y see the Kia Sportage the way they saw their generation: greater than the sum of its parts.

Cuties Oranges: Making Kid Orange-Eaters Different from Other Orange-Eaters

The campaign for Cuties Oranges is another example of how zeroing in on one business goal—in this case, protecting margins—led to work that strengthened the relationship between customer and product.

Linda Resnick is a brilliant ad woman. It was her idea to build a brand out of the small, sweet hybrid fruits called clementines, which are seedless and easy to peel. She named the brand Cuties.

At first my partner, Kim, and I created a bunch of ads that talked about the things that made Cuties different from other oranges or kids' snacks. We figured the job was to steal market share from grapes, oranges, bananas, and other fruits moms gave to kids. We designed spots that were about the benefits of sweet, seedless, and easy to peel—the things that made Cuties Cuties. But in reality, lots of fruit fit that profile.

Linda deserves credit for pointing out that the thing that makes Cuties really different from all other fruit is that *Cuties were made for kids.*

So we developed commercials about how Cuties and kids were made for each other. The ads needed to be inside jokes, as much about what made kids perfect for Cuties as what made Cuties perfect for kids. If we neglected to cement the relationship between Cuties and kids, most any clementine would do the job. We had to illustrate what makes one group of customers different from another.

The TV commercials were like video billboards. The first showed a bowl of Cuties on a kitchen counter. Suddenly a little hand reaches up from below the counter to take a Cutie from the bowl. The voice-over asks, "You know why Cuties are small? Because kids have small hands." Obvious. We signed the spots with the facts—seedless, sweet, E-Z peel—and the tagline "Kids love Cuties because Cuties are made for kids."

Another spot showed a six-year-old kid concentrating on peeling a Cutie. The voice-over asks, "You know why Cuties are easy to peel? So kids can peel them."

The idea to talk about Cuties in terms of what makes kids different—small hands, hating seeds, wanting to do things themselves (e.g., peeling), struck a chord. We were able to identify a specific audience (kids), and create a sense of mutual love and respect that resonated with parents as well. Most important, we protected the brand's margins. The season the campaign ran, Cuties sold out while other clementines were still available.

Carl's Jr.: The Customers We Couldn't Live Without

The first time I urged a client to transition to a mutual-love-and-respect type of campaign after years of running a successful differentiating campaign was when I worked on the Carl's Jr. account.

It's hard for an ad agency to move on from a successful campaign. Everybody involved has a different idea about why the current campaign works and what parts of it should be kept and what can be changed or abandoned. Everyone agreed, though, that our ad campaign celebrating the messy, drippy difference between Carl's Jr. burgers and everyone else's was no longer breaking through or building market share like it did when we started. The time had come to start making ads about what made our Carl's Jr. customers different from other fast-food customers.

During the time our campaign was running, new research emerged saying that the habits of heavy fast-food customers—the 20 percent of the market that accounts for 80 percent of sales—had changed. In 1986 the typical frequent fast-food user was defined as an eighteen-to-thirty-four-year-old male who ate a meal from a fast-food restaurant a couple of times a week. The new research defined them as guys who went to a fast-food restaurant more than *forty times a month*—every day and twice on some days.

For our guy, fast food was no longer a substitute for a home-cooked meal. At forty-plus visits a month, fast food was what these guys ate. They were not coming to Carl's Jr. or any other fast-food restaurant because they wanted a break from their ordinary routine of eating at home. They were coming for sustenance. Fast food was their cuisine.

Our new tactic was to let them know we needed them as much as they needed us. We could not survive without them: mutual love and respect.

The new commercials we created were not about the burgers; they were about the guys who needed the burgers. They featured guys in a supermarket, surrounded by different foods, but with no clue what to do with them. A spot called "Bread Aisle" featured twenty seconds of a guy completely overwhelmed by the hundreds of different breads to choose from. Too many choices. The guy was frozen like a deer in headlights. At the end of the commercial, while the guy continues to just stand there staring at all the different breads, the voice-over says, "The Carl's Jr. SuperStar. Without us, some guys would starve."

The ads drew comments like "You nailed my brother," "That's our son," or "That's me." To a lot of people, the spots meant nothing at all—just thirty seconds of a guy doing nothing in a supermarket—but not being for everybody was exactly the point.

Going Negative in a Zero-Sum Game

Years ago, I heard an NPR story about scientists doing research on animals in the Amazon rain forest. They found that any animal will heed the warning call of any other animal, regardless of species.

If a jaguar is near and a monkey screams in monkey-speak, "Hey! Danger! Danger! There's a jaguar—get out of here!" not only monkeys, but also toucans and deer and any other jaguar prey that heard the warning will clear the area. In the jungle, the researchers found, warnings are universally understood and obeyed.

However, things work differently when it comes to the "all clear" signal. Unlike warnings, the "Everything's cool, it's safe to come out now" cry is not universal. In fact, it's listened to and heeded only by animals of the same species. Monkeys will trust only other monkeys, toucans trust only other toucans, and so on.

Everyone says they hate negative ads, but there's a reason they work in advertising, politics, and other zero-sum situations. Negative ads work because people behave like animals.

Everyone says they hate negative ads, but there's a reason they work in advertising, politics, and other zero-sum situations. Negative ads work because people behave like animals.

In focus groups, few people admit to being influenced by negative advertising. In the real world, away from the controlled "best behavior" environment of focus groups, people respond to negative advertising the same way animals respond to warnings in the jungle. Everyone pays attention. Likewise, when it comes to a positive recommendation or endorsement, people trust only their own kind.

Take the case of political advertising. An election is a zero-sum game: The number of people who can vote is a fixed and known number, so a vote for one candidate is the same as a vote against the others. An electorate is made up of many different constituencies—or "species" of voters—with their own diverse backgrounds, wants, and needs.

People who create communications for elections can run a positive campaign and convince voters that the candidate is one of them—a trusted member of their species. Or they can go negative and warn everyone about the dangers of the other guy. If the law of the jungle holds true, everyone will believe the negative warning, regardless of where it comes from.

A great example of this is the smearing of John Kerry in the 2004 presidential election. Kerry was a wealthy U.S. senator, a Vietnam veteran, and a three-time Purple Heart recipient. But his campaign never recovered from the negative ads run against him by the "Swift Boat Veterans for Truth." Who? Exactly. Why would people believe the warnings about the character of a U.S. senator, veteran, and war hero coming from a group they had never heard of? Because like the animals of the rain forest, we're wired to heed warnings.

I once created an ad campaign for Whole Foods

Markets that succeeded by going negative in another kind of zero-sum environment.

Folks Gotta Eat

In 1993, Whole Foods came to Los Angeles and acquired a local health food chain called Mrs. Gooch's. Over the next several months, the newcomers changed the store signage stock and the description of the products from "health food" to "natural food." A year later, after the rollout was complete, customers were leaving en masse.

The problem was that Mrs. Gooch was not some made-up marketing gimmick like Mrs. Butterworth or the Pepperidge Farm man. Sandy Gooch was a Los Angeles schoolteacher, whose child had severe allergies. Her stores and the food she put in them began as a solution to her child's health problems. She didn't sell sugar or chocolate. People knew that if the food was good enough for Sandy's child, it was good enough for their family, too. They didn't know Whole Foods Markets from squat. So when they started to put "natural chocolates" and "natural sugar" on the shelves of the former Mrs. Gooch's, shoppers were unhappy.

In 1997, I was the creative director of an ad agency called Italia/Gal when we got a call from Joe Dobrow, the marketing manager at Whole Foods. The company's founder and CEO, John Mackey, didn't think much of advertising, but Joe did, and he was looking for an ad agency to help reintroduce Whole Foods Markets to the people of Los Angeles. They had $500,000 for a six-month campaign. The big Southern California grocery-store chains, like Vons, Ralphs, and Gelson's, spent combined about $150 million a year on advertising.

Joe explained that Whole Foods had done a poor job of preparing Mrs. Gooch's customers for the transition from "health food" to "natural food." I asked him to explain the concept of "natural food." Joe replied, "You know when you go to Ralphs and you pick up a chicken, how it's yellow?"

"Sure, I've bought chicken at Ralphs."

Joe said, "Chickens aren't yellow. Corn-fed chickens are white." He explained that conventional grocery-store chickens are yellow because they've been fed cheap marigold seeds instead of nutritious corn. He told me about their grass-fed beef, raised without hormones or antibiotics. He told us that conventional markets bathe fish in chlorine and sulfites to keep it looking fresh so people can't see and smell that it isn't. It was a very interesting—and very unappetizing—meeting.

Whole Foods Markets had a good product and a good story to tell. But their tiny budget in the face of the competition's huge one made this extremely challenging. I didn't want to say no to the assignment. To be honest, the problem seemed too interesting. They gave us a week to think about it and get back to them.

That weekend, I went grocery shopping at my local Ralphs, and when I reached for a package of chicken, I froze. Until that moment, the idea that when I eat an animal, I eat what the animal ate, had never crossed my mind. But there I was holding a chicken that had been raised on cheap marigold seeds, and it was grossing me out. I knew right then what we could do for Whole Foods.

Rather than convincing people that natural food was good for them, we ran an advertising campaign explaining why conventional food was at best disgusting and at worst poison.

We figured that food in Los Angeles is a zero-sum game. People have to eat; they have to get their food somewhere. If we could poison the well and make just 1 or 2 percent of food shoppers lose their appetite for conventional groceries the same way I lost mine, we would pack Whole Food Markets.

We decided that we wouldn't appear where traditional grocers advertised. Instead of buying pages in the *Los Angeles Times* Wednesday Food supplement, we bought the back page of the paper's Thursday Calendar section for twelve weeks. We ran print ads raising questions about the awful things other grocers did to sell unnatural yet conventional meat, fish, chicken, and groceries to innocent, unsuspecting Angelenos.

One headline asked, "Are you paying for hormones and steroids when what you really want is beef?" The Fourth of July ad read, "Baseball, hot dogs, apple pie, and nitrates?" We came up with a radio campaign featuring sixty-second commercials with only twenty seconds of copy. The Whole Foods spokesperson explained to the radio engineer that he had only twenty seconds of stuff to say because unlike regular grocery stores, Whole Foods Markets didn't sell additives or fillers. The spots started with an announcement about natural food for sale at Whole Foods Markets, followed by dead air, then a few facts about unappetizing conventional grocery practices, then more dead air, and finally the tagline: Pure food. That's the Whole story.

It all worked just the way we thought it would, because people are animals. Inside of just twelve weeks, the numbers had turned around. Whole Foods Markets customer counts were trending in the right direction for the first time since the acquisition of Mrs. Gooch's.

According to store managers, the best part was that what we called negative advertising was not perceived as negative at all by Whole Foods customers. They came into the stores holding the ads in their hands and told the store managers how much they appreciated the straight talk and honest information. It was no surprise to us. Hey, who doesn't appreciate a good warning? It's the law of the jungle.

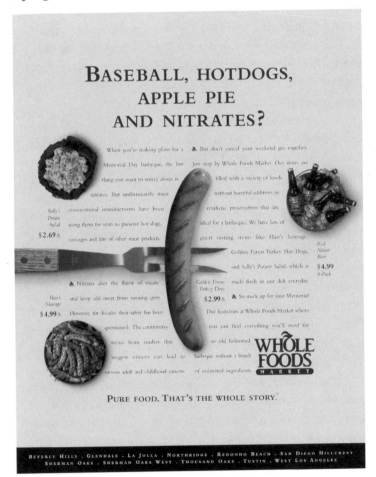

Surviving When Outgunned and Surrounded

A couple of times, I've developed communications solutions by taking a competitor's advantage and twisting it into a negative. It's sort of like a jujitsu tactic: Turn your opponent's power, size, or weight against him.

Friends of mine, Rich Cundiff and his wife, Lauren, were hard-core foodies who left L.A. and their high-profile, high-pressure jobs at a big national natural food market and moved about a hundred miles north to the little town of Los Olivos in the Santa Ynez Valley. They bought a small spread with room for 2,600 olive trees, and they also bought a roadside bodega. Their plan was to make high-quality olive oil and turn the little market into an old-fashioned type of food store, what people used to call a "staple and fancy." Instead of stocking the large variety of fine food items that you'd find at a gourmet specialty market, Los Olivos Grocery stocked just two brands in every category, one staple, quality everyday brand and one fancy, top-of-the-line brand. On the same shelf you might see Wesson corn oil right next to Gocce di Tartufo Bianco white truffle oil imported from Italy. The problem was how to get the locals who had driven past this little grocery store for years to stop in and see what it was like now. Not only was it different from what it used to be; it was different from any other market within a twenty-five-mile radius.

All the big markets surrounding the little Los Olivos Grocery had the advantage of being huge and well stocked. The flip side of that advantage is that all that space and inventory means it takes time to find items you are looking for. And when you do find what you are looking for, you may have to spend time making choices and thinking about what specific item is best for you.

For the Los Olivos Grocery to survive and thrive, its ad campaign would need to turn the little market into the Santa Ynez Valley's answer to the far-flung and confusing shopping problem with those surrounding big markets.

A Small Budget and a Big Attitude

We started out by creating ads that were all about the small size of the store. In the little Santa Ynez Valley local newspaper, we ran an ad featuring a photograph of an actual-size baguette. It was twenty-two inches high and took up three whole columns of a page from top to bottom. The ad read:

The new Los Olivos Grocery is small. It's 60 feet by 90 feet. But we devote 3 square feet to Anacapa bread because Anacapa bakes, and delivers daily, the very best traditional

*artisan bread we tasted. And Los Olivos Grocery has no
room for mediocrity. Los Olivos Grocery. Staple and Fancy.
And Nothing In Between.*

Next we ran a twelve-inch-wide by seven-inch-high
ad for meat, which was accompanied by a photograph of
a life-size tri-tip roast. The copy read:

*The new Los Olivos Grocery is small. It's 60 feet by 90 feet.
There is room enough, however, for the highest grade beef
available in the Valley. Top 1/3-Certified Angus Choice
Tri-Tips. New York Steaks. Rib-eyes. And fillets, to mention a few. Because at Los Olivos Grocery, we have room
for the most tender, most flavorful cuts of beef. But no room
for mediocrity. Los Olivos Grocery. Staple and Fancy. And
Nothing in Between.*

When Rich wanted to run ads about his new cheese
case, we created three cheese ads, each with a photo of an
actual-size hunk of cheese. Then we placed all three ads
on facing pages of the local newspaper. We made it look
as though cheese had taken over the valley.

Within two weeks, residents of the idyllic California
valley adopted the copy line "No room for mediocrity!" as
their own, proclaiming it with a wink when they chose
any upgrade. They knew exactly what the grocery store
was about.

Rich ran the campaign before high-speed broadband
made it possible to include online ads with large image
files in rural places like Los Olivos and the Santa Ynez
Valley. Nevertheless, the disruptive principle of actual-
size images of meat, vegetables, cheese, and bread would
work just as well on a webpage today as it did back then
in a newspaper.

We are used to seeing photos of things in newspapers and on webpages that are scaled down to fit the page. When the images are not scaled down to fit, they disrupt and disorient, raising a question in the mind of the reader, much as the small VW bug surrounded by white space did in *Life* magazine more than fifty years ago. An actual-size photo of a wheel of Brie in a local newspaper raised a question: What's with the big cheese? Ah—big cheese, small market. I get it.

The new Los Olivos Grocery is small. It's 60 feet by 90 feet. There's room enough, however, for the highest-grade beef available in the valley. Top 1/3 Certified Angus Choice

Tri-Tips. New York Steaks. Rib-eyes. And filets, to mention a few. Because at Los Olivos Grocery, we have room for the most tender, most flavorful cuts of beef. But no room for mediocrity.

Staple and Fancy. And Nothing In Between.

How Low Can You Go?

In the late 1990s, I worked on a million-dollar campaign to advertise Green Burrito for one year in the L.A. market. Taco Bell, the leader in the Mexican fast-food category, was spending fifteen times that amount in L.A. alone.

The day after our first meeting with the client, four of us from the agency drove to the nearest Green Burrito for lunch and discovered that the place was not yet ready for prime time. The restaurant, menu, and food left a lot to be desired. Much of the food was premade and heated up in a microwave. At best, this stuff kind of *reminded* you of Mexican food.

We came back and suggested that the Green Burrito folks use their million-dollar advertising budget to improve their menu. We tried to talk them out of advertising altogether until they had something—even one thing—they could brag about. But Green Burrito wouldn't be swayed and demanded we show them an advertising campaign.

It seemed the agency was in a no-win situation. What do we do? We knew what we didn't want to do: create advertising that would bump sales by promising delicious food. Luring people into the place, only to have an awful experience, would be a disaster. We knew that if people went in there and tried the food, they might never go back.

Instead we created commercials that left out the food, the place, the price, any hint of satisfied people, even a unique selling proposition. The spots featured a singing green dot floating on a black background. I created the green dot on twelve PowerPoint slides, which I animated by pressing the Advance button on the computer as fast as I could. These are some of the lyrics the dot sang:

Green Burrito is neat-o

Green Burrito good to eat-o

Green Burrito can't be beat-o

Green Burrito smell my feet-o

Green Green Green Burrito

Green Green Green Burrito

Green Burrito

It's good.

The animated spokesdot also delivered ten-second billboard spots that went:

If it's green, it's good.

If it's bluish-green, you're going to need shots.

Green Burrito

It's good.

We didn't leave stuff out of Green Burrito ads to make people curious. We left stuff out because nothing about the product was ready to be touted. When we created the Green Burrito "It's Good" campaign, the average television commercial cost somewhere between $150,000 and $200,000 to make. We created thirty-six Green Burrito commercials for a total production budget of $7,000.

After one year of advertising, Green Burrito's singing green dot achieved parity awareness with Taco Bell among eighteen- to thirty-six-year-old males. Better still, we bought Green Burrito enough time to work on the menu and food before creating ads inviting people in to experience a new and improved Green Burrito.

By making the ads on the cheap and singing about smelly feet and the possibility of infection, the advertising set customers' expectations so low that an actual Green Burrito experience could either meet or exceed them. They worked because, in a weird and extreme way, creating happy customers is a lot more about aligning expectations with product reality than it is about product quality.

What the Hell Do We Do if Something Goes Right?

It's not easy for an ad agency, let alone a single person, to come up with a communications campaign that does the job. To succeed, the campaign needs to get a lot right. It needs to: Zero in on the key consumer question that needs answering. Develop a breakthrough message that transfers the facts and evokes the emotions needed to get the job done. Align the interests and efforts of all clients and agency people involved. Develop a media plan that fits the message and finds the target. Pay attention to the metric of success that corresponds to the chosen business goal. And execute everything within the confines of a limited budget and time.

It's even harder to move from a successful campaign that gets it all right to a new message effort that requires a whole new set of ideas, answers, plans, and executions.

After an introductory campaign has been successful—that is, when inquiries are up—the wise thing to do is to run a limited-time offer to persuade some of those curious people to become regular paying customers. Remember, limited-time offers are designed to *temporarily* bump traffic, trials, or sales by encouraging people to sample some of the satisfaction that will be theirs if and when they decide to commit to an ongoing relationship with the product or service. When the audience reaches that point, the advertiser needs to switch gears again and move toward a differentiating campaign. This is when the product has become so familiar to people that if and when they decide that the product is right for them, its name is right there in the forefront of their minds.

Even if a campaign succeeds at differentiating a product effectively and memorably, however, eventually the marginal gains of sending another differentiating message to people who know a company well and like their products a lot becomes useless at best and annoying at worst. Why? By this time, the product and prospect are in a relationship. There's no need for a company to keep selling to the converted. It's time to move from a communication strategy that focuses on increasing market share by way of product differentiation to a strategy that protects or increases margins by creating feelings of mutual love and respect with customers. It's the point in the relationship when a company needs to say, "Enough about me and what makes me special; let's talk about you and why you and I are made for each other."

To keep the relationship interesting for the consumer receiving the messages and to keep business vital for the company sending the message, the sender needs to stay ahead of the curve, a little in front of what the receiver is ready for. Each different phase of a product, service, company, or customer communications relationship can be as short as a single media cycle or as long as decades. It depends on the product or service. But to keep the relationship going, companies have to stop doing what worked in one stage and commit to different methods and messages that are needed to succeed at the next. Companies need to stop sending messages that customers have received and internalized and move on to new information.

Apple illustrated this beautifully with their advertising campaigns for the Macintosh. To my mind, the introductory ad for the Apple Macintosh was the biggest advertising success of all time. The 1984 commercial showed an Orwellian vision of the future in which Big Brother (representing IBM, or top-down centralized computing power) had taken over people's minds. The bleak world is disrupted by a sledgehammer-wielding woman representing freedom and the power of personal computing. As the woman's hammer shatters the wall-size image of Big Brother, a voice-over announces, "On January 24th, Apple Computer will introduce Macintosh. And you'll see why 1984 won't be like '1984.'"

The cinematic Super Bowl showstopper was a brilliant piece of work designed to make people curious enough to inquire about Apple's new product, but the thing I liked even better was discovering that the ad was followed up by an elegantly simple limited-time-only campaign urging people to come in and "Test Drive a New Macintosh." The agency followed a big intro that made people curious with a limited-time offer to generate traffic. Then Apple and their ad agency followed the LTO with ten years of differentiating ads that explained why a Mac was "The Computer for the Rest of Us." After ten years of ads about what made Macs different, they developed a mutual-love-and-respect campaign that celebrated what made Mac users unique: "Think Different."

The progression of these messaging campaigns made me feel more confident about the model of the four kinds of ads I carried around in my pocket. A big part of what made the model helpful to me was the rationale for moving off of one kind of message and onto another. Act One: introduction; Act Two: trial; and so on. I could see why, when businesses didn't move on, they'd run into trouble.

One of the most notorious advertising screwups was the 1990 introduction of the Infiniti Q45. Just as Apple left the actual Mac computer out of the introduction ads, Infiniti made people curious to see its new car by leaving it out of their first introductory ads. Instead of showing the new Q45, the commercials showed images of waves, rocks, and trees. Inquiries skyrocketed as people talked about the ads, which focused on Infiniti's unique philosophy about making cars. But unlike Apple, Infiniti failed to follow that successful curiosity-evoking introductory ad campaign with a limited-time offer to get people into dealerships to try the product. Instead, they followed with more spots featuring more images of natural objects and textures and more copy talking car-design philosophy. Repeating a successful Act One made for a dismal Act Two. In just six months, Infiniti went from looking brave and bold enough to take a big risk to looking tentative and afraid to move on. The brand never recovered from its initial miscalculation.

Claude Shannon, the mathematician and engineer, said, "Information is a message that reduces doubt."

Claude Shannon, the mathematician and engineer, said, "Information is a message that reduces doubt." The better we understand this, the better able we are to wrap our heads around an interesting conundrum: The better a message works the first time, the worse it will work the next time. The more a message successfully reduces doubt, the less doubt there is to reduce.

The most successful artists, writers, generals, executives, directors, and doctors are good at not relying on what worked last time, at not fighting the last war. The great communicators know how to move on at the right time.

Part Three
Secret Motives, Agendas, Traps, and Techniques

Choose, Align, Anticipate

For years, I carried around a written summary of my advertising messaging model in my pocket and stared at it often. I stared at it when I got a new assignment to develop an ad. I stared at it when I had to pitch a new piece of business. I stared at it whenever I saw an ad I liked or a campaign that caught my attention. They say when you have a hammer, everything looks like a nail—and they're right.

I tried to poke holes in my model. I looked at the successes and failures of campaigns created by others to see if they, too, fit the pattern: curiosity for inquiries; limited-time offers to temporarily bump sales or trials; increasing market share by defining a product or service's most memorable differences; and protecting margins through mutual-love-and-respect ads that cement customer relationships.

Over time, I noticed that the successful companies I admired, the ones that did great advertising, seemed to adhere to the principles of the model. Nike is a great example. It was among the best at using celebrity athletes to distinguish what made Nikes different from other athletic shoes. Their "Find Your Greatness" spot featuring an overweight boy jogging takes their mutually shared values message even further by demonstrating that Nike cares about and understands runners to a degree no other company can.

In contrast, struggling companies often do one kind of ad again and again. Think about mattress companies that are always advertising price or fast food places stuck in a tactical cycle of constantly introducing new products. It's as though the brand journey of these companies has come to standstill.

I realized from the examples of successful advertisers that my model helped me do three things a lot better than I did them before:

- Choose a single business goal for every message.
- Align messaging, audiences, and media strategy—plus the resources and expectations of everyone involved.
- Anticipate, and explain what to do next, after what works now stops working.

This section is about the practical ins and outs of understanding and aligning people's interests, anticipating what to tell people once a message gets through loud and clear, and how to persuade face-to-face.

Bottom Line or Top Line?

Nothing has a greater impact on a persuasive message than the motives of the person or business sending it.

According to Alfred P. Sloan Jr., longtime president, chairman, and CEO of General Motors Corporation, the purpose of business is to make profits. In the opinion of the famous American management consultant Peter F. Drucker, however, the purpose of business is to create happy customers.

Whether you're creating persuasive messages for clients, businesses, products, services, or even yourself, it's important to know if the message sender is motivated by making profits or by making happy customers.

The "make profits" people, like Sloan, are all about the bottom line, how much money a business gets to keep after all other expenses are accounted for. They see advertising as a cost that needs to be quantified and justified. The "make happy customers" people, like Drucker, focus on the top line—the line on the ledger that shows sales, or how much money customers are willing to fork over for a company's products and services. They tend to see advertising as an investment in a way of interacting with others that defies a dollar value—like a smile or an attitude. In my experience, the bottom-line people tend to be

The purpose of business is to make profits. The purpose of business is to create happy customers. Who's right?

The messages I've created for bottom-line people are usually about driving incremental, measurable results.

more solitary and cerebral. The happy-customers people, on the other hand, tend to see advertising and marketing as a way to do what they love best: connecting with and attracting people.

I find that often it helps to put a contemporary face on the people who represent the "making profits" and "making happy customers" points of view. For example, when I think of a person who believes the purpose of business is to make a profit, I think of Mitt Romney. When I think of a person who believes the purpose of business is to make a happy customer, I picture Steve Jobs.

The Steve Jobses of the world want to make insanely great products, because regardless of how they treat others, they really are "people" people. They relish the spotlight, they enjoy presenting to a crowd, connecting, screaming, and mixing it up. They are emotional beings. Connections—both good and bad—are at their core. When reading Walter Isaacson's biography *Jobs,* I was struck by the number of times he describes Steve Jobs bursting into tears. Rightly or wrongly, he took his products, services, and business personally. Top-line people—showmen, promoters, and impresarios like Jobs—value imagination, innovation, novelty, and surprise.

The Mitt Romneys—those who are in business to make profits—seem to be less attached to companies and individual products. They are at their best when moving from problem to problem and working to create measurable results. They tend to be more methodical in their thinking and highly motivated by returns on investment. In terms of measurability, bottom-line folks value predictability and repeatable results.

So who's right?

Both sides have their merits, but one thing is clear:

Considering what a client or company expects to get as a result of their advertising or communicating without first considering what the client or company expects to get as a result of doing business is missing the forest for the trees. Plus, the two different measures of success—bottom line or top line—lead to two very different kinds of communication.

The messages I've created for bottom-line people are usually about driving incremental, measurable results. They are filled with facts and features and dates and times. These messages are designed to attract more customers, make the phone lines light up, crash the servers, put asses in seats, and fill the boat, hotel, or stadium. Bottom-line people love messages about scarcity and urgency and special prices, promotional codes, and "while supplies last." They especially love the quantifiable results they can get from this type of advertising.

The messages I've created for top-line, "make happy customers" people are more about creating an emotional connection with customers. Ads for hamburgers, cars, and software are stories filled with emotion and humor designed to evoke feelings of familiarity, pride, and distinction. The happy-customers people invest in communications that fill their businesses, products, and services with personality. Memorability, beauty, trustworthiness, and empathy are just some of the human characteristics that top-liners use to make customers happy.

Two types of motivation, two types of advertising. That's why in the early stages of a project, it never hurts to ask the question, "Are we doing this to grow the top or the bottom line?" just to see how the people you're working with respond. What drives them is what drives them—it's not right or wrong. But it's up to you to figure it out before you start spinning your wheels.

The messages I've created for top-line, "make happy customers" people are about creating an emotional connection with customers.

What's My Motivation?

On my first day as the advertising consultant on *Mad Men,* I walked in with a chart that illustrated the motivations behind the key people working in an ad agency. I wanted the writing staff to understand the three very different jobs done by ad agency higher-ups and how the jobs themselves can motivate the people doing them to work with— or against—each other.

One area of the chart featured the account executives, the agents and salespeople who act as a liaison between the client and the agency. These are the people who manage the client's advertising business, as well as the client's expectations. If what the account executive has promised the customer costs too much to deliver, the agency doesn't make money. Worse, the unhappy client could leave and the agency goes out of business. In terms of motivation, account people fall into the "making profits" camp.

Another area of the chart included copywriters and art directors—the creatives who develop and produce ads and advertising campaigns. In other businesses, these people are the operations team, the skilled pros who make the products and services that the company sells. A great writer or art director can be what the army calls a force multiplier. They can come up with ideas that make a $2-million budget work like $10 million. Creatives are motivated by a desire to master their chosen craft. Creative control, peer recognition, praise, and the approval of other professionals go a long way with them. These are definitely "make happy customers" folks.

Media buyers made up the third section of the chart. Reaching the largest audience for the least amount of money is their job. Media people are definitely focused on keeping costs down and making profits. Whereas account executives are like Hollywood agents who need to be sensitive to the customer's expectations while representing the interests of the client and agency, media people are more like corporate litigators. They play a zero-sum game: They have a fixed budget to work with, and the people they buy from have a fixed inventory of space and time. Media people get what they negotiate. Like a lot of people who bargain for a living, they are motivated by a desire to beat the salesperson on the other end of the phone line.

With the help of my chart, I tried to show that what makes an ad agency a dramatic and dynamic place is not the nature of each different job. What makes an agency dramatic and dynamic is the clash of different *motivations* and the never-ending struggle to meet and exceed always-changing expectations.

Not everyone who comes to the table to help craft and send a persuasive message has the same agenda. Messages get muddled, and we get in trouble when we take it for granted that we all have the same motivations.

Stories about what messages can accomplish when everybody on the team is on the same page and stories about how efforts can go awry when people working together have different agendas are part of what made *Mad Men* relatable and contemporary. The show's writers did a brilliant job of taking these various motives and bringing them to life through believable and meticulously crafted stories of multidimensional characters engaged in both cooperation and conflict.

Big Ideas, Killer Ideas, and Big Idea Killers

Ideas can inspire change, bring down governments, cure diseases, connect people, and spread like wildfire. They can also compete with other ideas to win hearts, minds, and dollars. And then there's the most persuasive idea of all: the Big Idea.

People often talk about the Big Idea in ad agencies, communication firms, publishing houses, software companies, TV networks, and other places where ideas are generated. Over the years, I've heard a lot of definitions of a Big Idea. One way to recognize one is by the feeling you get when you see it. You wish you had thought of it. I've read that a Big Idea makes possibilities explode in your head when you see it. Legendary ad man George Lois said, "A Big Idea spreads like poison gas."

I have two problems with most of these definitions. The first is that *big* is a relative term. The second is the big pressure that comes with the word *big*. In my experience, it's hard to think of any idea, let alone a big one. And the bigger the idea the client, agency, or boss wants me to come up with, the emptier my head gets. If someone says, "If we don't come up with a really Big Idea, we could lose this account," I will spend three days staring at a blank page without a single thought in my head. "We need a Big Idea" guarantees white noise. So I came up with my own definition: A Big Idea is one that can beat or kill a smaller idea.

Take this example. Two guys walking through the woods come upon a bear. The bear is big and mean-looking. As the bear turns and starts lumbering toward the two guys, one of them starts to take off his hiking boots. The second guy says, "Are you crazy? You can't outrun a bear." The first guy says, "I don't need to outrun the bear. I just need to outrun you."

The "Think Small" ad for the newly introduced 1959 Volkswagen Bug, created by advertising agency Doyle Dane Bernbach, was a Big Idea. Why? It killed the Detroit auto industry's accepted wisdom that, when it comes to cars, bigger is always better.

I think my definition is freeing, because I no longer have to come up with a Big Idea. I just need to find one that's bigger than the other guy's.

When looking for Big Ideas, try coming up with small ways to ding the competition.

In 1994, McDonald's was spending billions advertising their one-dollar value menu. At Carl's Jr., we started advertising a huge burger called the SuperStar that cost almost three bucks. For about five years, Carl's ran successful ads that featured nothing but big, expensive SuperStars. McDonald's couldn't do a thing; they were too invested in their low-cost message. "Big and expensive" was McDonald's weakness. Advertising a huge, expensive burger was a Big Idea for Carl's because it was a small way to chisel away at the foundation the competition's business was built on: an inexpensive, one-dollar menu.

110

Another way I come up with ideas is to think about how to throw a wrench into the day of someone working at my biggest competitor. To me, businesses, big or small, are intimidating. People that I'm similar to, like marketing executives or other creative directors, are not. Finding something to say that demands a response can get ideas flowing. I love thinking about what it would take to turn the day of the creative director at my biggest competitor's ad company to hell. I think, "What could I say or show in an ad that would upset the apple cart?" I picture that creative director running through the office waving a fresh printout of my ad in her hand and screaming, "Can they do this? Can they say this? Call our lawyers! How do we get this to stop?" Then I think to myself, "What's in that ad that gets that person so upset?" I may never actually run it, but thinking about it often sends me in the right direction.

When I began working in advertising, in the mid-1980s, I was assigned to a fast-food account. When the creative teams would strategize or present ideas, we would sometimes talk about our client's products, but we talked a lot more about ways to beat the competition. If they closed at 10:00 p.m., we'd talk about staying open till midnight. If five dollars bought you a pound of food over there, we'd talk about ways to make five dollars get you a pound and a half at our place.

In the 1980s there was a cola war between Coke and Pepsi and a burger war between McDonald's and Burger King, and you got the sense that competition between the rivals was fierce and serious. Then suddenly everything changed. I started working with more people who were brought up believing that a positive self-image is more important to success than besting the competition. The stronger that belief, the less competitive the work.

> When looking for Big Ideas, try coming up with small ways to ding the competition.

By 2001, the clients I worked with seemed to have developed a real aversion to thinking and talking about their competition—not just my fast-food clients but all my clients in all sorts of categories. At first I heard companies talk as if their competition didn't matter. "We plan on growing organically," they said, meaning they didn't need to do unseemly things like steal customers from competitors.

A couple of years ago, some clients told me that they wanted to be the "iPhone of copier papers." They had top-of-the-line copy paper, responsibly harvested from sustainable forests. But anyone who's been to Staples or Office Depot or watched *The Office* knows the shelves are stacked with different papers competing for copier-paper dollars. It wasn't that they wanted to be the "iPhone of copier paper" that struck me. That was just a young marketing person's way of saying she wanted her product to be cool. The thing that really struck me was the magical thinking. All the talk was about who the paper company wanted to be. There was no talk at all about the competition—whom the company had to outrun to avoid being eaten by the bear. They didn't grasp that the communications business is a game of confrontation, like wrestling, not a game of presentation and pageantry, like bodybuilding.

There's a saying in Hollywood that a hero is only as good as a villain is bad. Having another idea to triumph over may help you generate stronger, more competitive ideas. David may be a good idea. But David beating Goliath? That's a Big Idea.

Advertising Is a Toolbox: Pick a Tool

People who are skilled in the practical art of advertising (using the toolbox) have learned from experience which kind of advertising (tool) will likely work best to accomplish a particular business goal or solve a marketing problem. Yet the message that works best in every case is the message with one well-defined goal that knows exactly what it's being sent out in the world to do.

Is your message intended to announce a new product? Attract an audience to a blog or personal YouTube channel? Move cars off the lot? Differentiate your catering concept from your competitor's? Protect margins with an image ad that resonates particularly well with loyal, enthusiastic customers? Each of these goals requires a very different kind of *message, media strategy,* and, depending on the industry and the competitive environment, a very different *budget.*

For example, for the small price of an Internet connection, an ad on Craigslist can help a person get rid of an ugly nightstand taking up room in the garage. Craigslist is a hard, fact-based communication environment. Where is the thing? What's the price? Is it still available? Craigslist is big on logistical local opportunity but not real big on emotional appeal or an ongoing relationship with the advertiser. The goal is simple: to move the merchandise ASAP and make money while you're at it. As countless Craigslist sellers can tell you, this tool works.

By the same token, one can spend five years and hundreds of millions of media and production dollars to produce and run a multimedia campaign using many different advertising messages and turn a dusty, old fast-food franchise into the one place hungry eighteen- to thirty-four-year-old males head for when they want a big, juicy hamburger. In this case, the goal was to increase the company's market share in the large and very competitive fast-food market. The multimedia advertising tools used in this example worked well, too.

By far the hardest thing about marketing, advertising, or persuading is figuring out exactly what you want to see happen as a result of your specific efforts. Then you must commit wholeheartedly to that goal.

If you ask me, a person's willingness to commit to solving one particular problem at a time is what separates the pros from the "Does advertising work?" folks. I've heard loads of reasons why committing to doing just one thing at a time is impossible. When pressed to decide on a single communication strategy, a client once told me, "We have to advance in all directions at the same time." I told him I had never heard a better definition of standing still.

The Sizzle Sucks.
The Steak Rocks.

There's an old advertising adage: Sell the sizzle, not the steak. But what do you do when the sizzle's not so hot?

Sometimes the best way to change a brand or reputation is to change the promise, not the product.

Advertisers have been repositioning products for years. Take the case of Marlboro, which was famously introduced and marketed as a "ladies' cigarette." When that idea went nowhere, it was time for Marlboro to rethink its strategy. It found a rough-hewn actor, bought a cowboy hat and some chaps, added a couple of horses and a wide-open range, and voilà: The Marlboro Man was born. More recently, Burberry transformed itself from a maker of stodgy English raincoats to an international trend-setting sportswear brand.

A company will often ask several ad agencies to show it what a new ad could do for its business. Each of the resulting proposals is called a pitch. For most pitches, the agencies are told whether or not the client is interested in ideas that change the promise only, the promise and the product, or neither. Sometimes the company wants to

Sometimes the best way to change a brand or reputation is to change the promise, not the product.

keep its communication strategy the same; it just wants to see how other agencies would execute it.

By far the most successful advertising campaign I've ever been part of did nothing but change the promise the company made to the market. The change made the promise more honest and, most important, more primal.

For fifteen years, Carl's Jr. had been offering a clean, wholesome, McDonald's kind of promise. Like McDonald's, Carl's Jr. ads showed a big, nicely stacked burger on TV. Unlike McDonald's, however, Carl's Jr. would then deliver a charbroiled product that looked like a sloppy, drippy mess. Naturally, this dissonance was a problem for the company's reputation.

But the ad agency—Mendelsohn/Zien—convinced Carl's Jr. that its customers, eighteen- to thirty-four-year-old hungry guys, wanted a burger more like the messy, drippy thing Carl's was delivering at the drive-through window. The agency created a Carl's Jr. burger campaign that loudly declared, "If it doesn't get all over the place, it doesn't belong in your face." The new TV commercials showed big, messy burgers. All the company had to do to deliver on the new promise was to not change a thing. The burgers at the window looked just like the ones promised on TV, and business went through the roof.

Sooner or later, every persuader encounters a product that doesn't measure up to its current promise or marketing strategy. When that happens, my advice is to take another look at it and try to come up with two or three other promises that it *can* make good on. There's no reason to keep trying to pound a square peg into a round hole. It's a lot easier to change the shape of the hole.

No More Content for Me— I've Had Enough

I watch a lot of movies and read a lot of books. I spend two hours or more every day online reading news, doing research, conducting business, or buying stuff. In all that time, I have never once searched for content, spent time with content, or recommended content to a friend. I don't know anyone else who has, either.

Nobody covets content. Nobody waits in line to see content. Nobody dreams of growing up and accepting an award for Best Content. And nobody tattoos content on their body. That's because content and messages are very different things.

Content is generated by, uploaded to, posted to, linked to, or aggregated by digital media networks for the purpose of increasing the size of the network. The producers of content do not consider, respect, or exist for the people who use it. Their first obligation is to the network.

Conversely, a *message* is sent from one person to another. A message is a means of connecting. The creator of a message is responsible to both the sender and the receiver. A story, an image, or piece of music are all messages, sent with a sense of empathy for an audience of readers, spectators, or listeners.

Content is mindless. It's made up of features without a thought about the real benefits of a message: informing, entertaining, inspiring, or motivating.

My career in advertising taught me that communicating is about focusing on the benefits that consumers are buying, not the product features that companies are selling. Content is the sound bite, news clip, show, or other feature that's sold by big Information Age players like TV networks, advertisers, and aggregators. Benefits—the thrills, goosebumps, laughter, and understanding that people are hoping to get from their media choices—are virtually impossible to find in a content-driven world. If you need to fill a page with copy, then content will do, but if you want to truly motivate a human being, you need a gripping story or a work of art.

Content is another word for news, entertainment, and rhetoric that is made without talent, commitment, or experience. It includes entertainment presented by aggregators that simply regurgitate art or information that someone else has created. The same goes for much of the crowdsourced amusements you'll find on YouTube and other websites.

Persuasion relies on the ability to care about what your audience feels. It requires talent, commitment, and experience, which makes it far more valuable than content can be or will ever be. If you honestly want to communicate, inspire, attract, and seduce people, the first thing you need to do is to get rid of all the content that's attached to the project, the process, or the people involved. As you do, your problem, solutions, goals, and customers will become much clearer.

Persuasion is personal. It's a human endeavor. Content does not describe anything people desire, use, or want. It's stuff that machines can recognize, store, and move. It's perfectly fine with me if engineers and programmers use the word to explain what their system or app does, but I don't need words that describe what machines do getting in my way.

For years, engineering jargon has been working its way into the communications industry, as well as everyday life. Now these terms are all over the place: end user, interface, data dump, multitasking. Multitasking once referred to the simultaneous execution of more than one program by a single computer processor. That's fine for computer processors, but when people try to multitask, they end up doing a lot of things half-assed. Worse, asking consumers to "interface" or experience multiple "touch points" just sounds nasty. Engineerspeak, like content, devalues the things humans do and makes content seekers think they can conduct business with humans without using human talent. It doesn't work.

By far the fastest and easiest way to improve any communication designed to persuade people is by using words that describe what *people* do rather than words that describe what *machines* do. The first thing I do when I'm given a brief or assignment is go through it and remove all the words that describe what computers and machines do. Then I look at the brief again with an eye toward finding the most human thing I can about the product or service.

Briefings, business plans, and communication strategies that rely on people communicating like machines don't work because people do not communicate like

People communicate for two reasons: to transfer facts and to evoke emotions.

machines. Machines communicate for one reason only: to transfer facts or data. People communicate for two reasons: to transfer facts and to evoke emotions.

Real persuasion requires both. It must transfer real facts *and* make real emotional connections with real people. Where's the funny? What's sad? What's stupid or poetic or beautiful? Answering these questions goes beyond the scope of content. It requires sympathy, empathy, and *talent*. I once fought for a week to replace the word *hungry* on an advertising brief with the word *voracious*. Everybody gets hungry, but with a voracious appetite, things might get messy. Clothes could come off, dishes might get broken. Hungry can be dealt with. Voracious will likely cause a scene. The difference between hungry and voracious takes experience to understand, talent to convey, and commitment to fight for.

Informing, entertaining, or persuading requires effort and understanding. Providing content is more like providing lunch for the local advertising club. It's easy and cheap to procure and pass out, and it's not what anyone wants or will enjoy eating.

Effective communication requires knowing your audience and caring about their satisfaction. Without commitment to communicating something to an audience, all you've got is content. Content turns communication into a one-way street. If a tree falls in the forest and nobody's there to hear it, it makes a sound, but the sound is merely content, because no human has responded to it. At the end of a successful communication between a sender and a receiver, somebody expects to be informed or moved in some way. Referring to news, information, stories, and games as content eliminates the provider's personal responsibility for doing his job well and communicating effectively.

Referring to the stuff people create, sell, and distribute as content allows businesses to ignore customers' needs and the benefits that meet them. Real talent, experience, and commitment take real time and cost real money. I've never heard the words "Content is king" spoken by a genuine writer or artist. I've heard them only from online operators or aggregators who have figured out how to profit from presenting work they've never labored at or paid to create, produce, or distribute.

The more MBAs, lawyers, and venture capitalists involved in the advertising, communications, and entertainment businesses, the more I hear about content. They love the stuff. And the stuff they love most is "user-generated content." Judging from the level of enthusiasm, user-generated content is to online communication what Chateau Lafite Rothschild is to generic Bordeaux. It's the shit!

Lately so much soulless content has invaded my world that I feel the need to remind myself of the value of my work before every meeting. I imagine telling these aggregators and digital dynamos, "I'm an artist and a writer. If you want me to punch you in the throat, call what I make 'content.' It devalues what I do."

The job is about making a genuine connection with people, which requires real empathy and real talent—which are beyond the realm of content. If clients want to make this valuable connection, they should be willing to pay for it.

What's more, if you're not getting paid, you're not doing advertising. You're offering only an informed opinion, which gives your client and potential audience the permission to ignore it. To me, content providers are undiscriminating, uncaring, and cheap. I've got no use for them or the content they provide. Neither should you.

Three Reasons
to Take a Job; Pick Two

It's hard to make other people happy when the daily skirmishes, conflicts, misunderstandings, and hidden agendas that are part of the job are making you frustrated, anxious, or miserable. If you approach a job by setting your own expectations for what you'll get out of it, you'll have a better shot at knowing when your work meets or exceeds those expectations—and feel happier about doing it.

I've already said that it's important to take a step back to see what's motivating the company on whose behalf you're communicating. It's just as valuable to understand your own motivations for taking a job. It leads to a saner state of mind on both sides of the table.

There used to be a sign on the wall of every print shop I worked with that read: SPEED. QUALITY. PRICE. PICK ANY TWO. The sign was about the relationship of skill to time and money.

I believe there are essentially three reasons creative professionals accept work. The first is, of course, money.

The second is the opportunity to prove to a potential client or patron that you can do the job better—or more cheaply—than somebody else. And the third is to exercise creative control, which hopefully will lead to peer recognition and/or award-winning work.

Money.
Opportunity.
Control.
Pick any
two.

It's pretty damn rare when you can achieve all three. That's why I want to make a sign for creatives, writers, and artists that would hang in every advertising agency, design studio, writers' room, and agent's office. It would read: MONEY. OPPORTUNITY. CONTROL. PICK ANY TWO.

The key to a satisfying career as an artist, writer, or other creative professional is not doing award-winning work on every assignment, making a lot of money, or even building a huge list of clients. The key is knowing the reasons why you take a job and keeping those reasons in mind from start to finish. Happy, successful creative professionals have no problem doing this. In fact, many do it without even realizing it.

Unhappy, dissatisfied, or new-to-the-game creatives are another story. They tend to sign on to a job for opportunity or creative control and hope that by making the most of the opportunity and doing great work, they can inspire an enlightened and grateful client to pay them what they're actually worth later on. I've never seen it happen.

One of my favorite *Mad Men* episodes occurs in season two, when Peggy Olson is beginning her career, as a junior copywriter. She takes on a job for her church, assuming that because she has agreed to work for free, she will maintain creative control of the project. She assumes wrong. The priest, who is essentially her boss, has ideas he wants incorporated that Peggy does not agree with. I love this business story because everybody I know has agreed at some point in their career to work for free and fallen into the same trap. In those cases, they got one out of three—opportunity only.

From a client's point of view, nobody likes awarding a job for money and opportunity, then finding out that the person who took it wants money and creative control. The most successful relationships are based on motivations that work for both parties involved.

Money. Opportunity. Control. Settling for one is soul crushing. Get two, and you are doing business. Nobody gets all three.

Great Idea! Now Sell It!

There is a scene in the movie *A Few Good Men* in which Tom Cruise's character, a smart but cold defense attorney, yells in frustration at Demi Moore's character, his idealistic and passionate co-counsel, "It doesn't matter what I believe; it only matters what I can prove." In the world of persuasion, it doesn't matter how great your ideas are; it only matters what you can sell.

Selling your ideas is the process of figuring out how to make other people take ownership of them—how to make your ideas not *yours* anymore. To do this, you have to listen and include people and share credit with people to whom credit is not due. In the business of communications, professionals get paid both for their ideas and for letting customers in on how great it feels to contribute to the making of a powerful idea.

When I first started working in ad agencies, I was good at coming up with ideas long before I was good at presenting and selling them. I had a lot of good ideas and a lot of motivation, and nothing felt worse than watching a good idea die because I was a bad salesman.

In the world of persuasion, it doesn't matter how great your ideas are; it only matters what you can sell.

The sale is made when the salesperson has everyone agreeing to his appraisal of the problem at hand.

One reason Don Draper is so good in meetings is because I was so terrible. Almost everything I learned about being persuasive, I learned the hard way—on the job, surrounded by people with a lot of money riding on how well I did. It was a nerve-rattling way to learn. However, I discovered that high stakes and high anxiety can improve focus and clarity.

The Sale Is in the Setup

The setup to your presentation is the most important opportunity you'll have to win the room over to your way of thinking. You'll know you've done it when people start nodding in agreement about a general concept or universal principle before you show them a thing.

It doesn't matter what you're presenting—designs, commercials, posters, online ads, pop-up concepts, websites, or pitches for movies—you need to convince people to buy into and agree with the key principle or insight underlying your idea before you try to sell a specific way of illustrating or executing it. You need to go from "I'm here with a bunch of ideas I thought of for you" to "We all agree, based on our common experience, that what we see, do, or notice is shared by a lot of people who are not in this room."

Before going into any presentation, a good salesperson has prepared one good line, story, or insight designed to get everybody in the meeting nodding in agreement. It is at the point when the salesperson has everyone agreeing to his appraisal of the problem at hand that the sale is made. The rest is just polite theater.

Before Don Draper reveals to the men from Kodak what he thinks their new circular slide projector should be called, he gets them to agree to the general idea that everyone at one time or another longs for the past and would like to circle back and revisit it. Only after he has them nodding in agreement with that concept does he reveal the new name: Carousel.

Matt Weiner talks about that moment when Don or Peggy Olson gets the nod during the setup as the moment when they enter into a conspiracy with their clients. The technique is all over *Mad Men*. You see it when Don sells the Carousel commercial at the conclusion of season one. You see it when Peggy presents and sells a new tagline to the folks from Popsicle, a line that makes sharing frozen sugar water an almost religious experience: "Take it. Break it. Share it. Love it." You can also see it in her setup to the Burger Chef campaign in *Mad Men*'s final season. We never actually see Peggy present her idea. We don't need to. We knew that the meeting was a success and the agency won the business when we saw the clients nodding at her setup.

The people you're presenting to may not like your ideas for the same reasons you like them, but if you find a relevant general principle or insight on which everyone in the room can agree, you're halfway home.

Making You Work for You

My first creative director, Jim Walker, was the first person I ever saw present and sell ideas to clients. Jim comes from a small town in Oregon, where he played college football. He's clean-cut and good-looking and has a beautiful wife and family. He's also smart and creative and has a Will Rogers "Aw, shucks" way of talking about stuff that makes almost everything he says sound like either common sense or folk wisdom.

Not knowing there was any other way of doing it, I tried to present like Jim. Now, I'm stocky and swarthy. I look more like your friendly neighborhood Romanian anarchist than an all-American football hero. And I tend to have this seriously furrowed brow. Needless to say, Jim's folksy approach did not work for me.

My second boss is to this day the best presenter I have ever seen. Bruce Dundore is a huge guy who is built like the French actor Gérard Depardieu. Like Depardieu, Bruce has the stage presence of a great performer. He can make any story funny and spin the smallest observation into a twenty-minute one-man show. When he speaks, he uses his hands to illustrate and emphasize and conjure images in an almost primitive, hypnotic way. His presentations are funny, sweaty, take-no-prisoners dramatic happenings. I remember watching Bruce climb up onto a conference table and slither around like a 275-pound mutant lizard in front of two dozen guys in suits. He was trying to sell the idea of a talking iguana for a chain of Mexican restaurants. The man can sell anything. I tried to present like Bruce, and that didn't go so well, either.

Eventually I figured out that I had to make the worried brow work for me. It wasn't going anywhere, and I couldn't mask it with some other person's patter or mannerisms. I learned to honestly explain to clients that unless I brought in ideas based on sound reasoning and intelligent insight, I couldn't sleep at night. I told them that I took their problems seriously and internalized them. It's part of who I am. I presented ideas that were funny and dramatic and sometimes even melancholy—but there was always an underlying anxious edge to my presentations. That worked for me, because it's me. I do feel passionately about ideas, and I do have an edge. Some like my approach; others, not so much. Yet I learned to be okay with the way I observe the world, come up with ideas, and tell stories. It works for me.

So be yourself. The people you're presenting to may not always believe you, but they need to know that *you* believe you.

Show How the Idea Will Rock Their World

Jay Chiat, chairman of the advertising agency Chiat/Day, said, "Don't sell them who they are; sell them who they want to be." I would go further: If possible, use pictures and *show* them who they want to be.

I once worked for a software company that was in a protracted and complicated lawsuit. The company was a leader and innovator and was accustomed to regularly rolling out new products accompanied by huge industry fanfare. When they were sued, the *New York Times* and the *Wall Street Journal* ran unflattering stories about the company's ongoing legal battles every day for two years. Naturally, morale at the place was awful.

In the middle of all this, I was hired to help the company launch a new product. It was a good product, and I came up with an interesting way to introduce it. Instead of just walking in and presenting the idea, however, I dummied up a *New York Times* front page that showed what their world was going to look like the morning after the rollout. I Photoshopped a picture of the company's

CEO standing in Times Square with a big smile on his face as he held the product, surrounded by billboards advertising it in the background. Above the picture, a 200-point headline announced an end to the company's legal troubles and the dawning of a new day. I wrote a "news story" underneath, explaining how this new product was going to resurrect the company and change the business landscape.

None of it was true. None of it had happened. It was all just inexpensive, creative, emotionally charged visualization.

But during the presentation, the company's head of PR, the guy who for a year had been getting the crap kicked out of him by the press on a daily basis, couldn't take his eyes off the mocked up *New York Times*. Eventually he reached over, picked up the phony newspaper, clutched it to his chest, and sort of hugged it for the rest of the meeting. More than a successful new product launch, those people working at that company—and that PR guy in particular—just wanted to be in a world where they were the good guys again. When they saw a picture of that world, they bought our whole advertising program.

Most companies you're likely to work for will not be similarly embattled. Nevertheless, your task is always to show the people you are working for that you can see beyond their day-to-day trials and tribulations. Your task is to prove to the people you are working for that you know that the design and the products and the marketing and the advertising are all just the means to the company's ends. Their ultimate goal is to show the world the story they believe about themselves. Let them know you understand where they're trying to go and then show them how your idea, program, design, or communication

Your task is to show people that you see and understand their story and where they want to be.

131

piece furthers their story and helps them get from where they are to where they want to be.

There is an ad campaign for Swedish State Railway that I love. It's all about visualizing the emotional destination rather than the physical journey. It's a great example of selling rail travel by skipping the whole story about the train and the comfort and how you get there and instead going right to the happy ending, the reason people travel by trains in the first place. And by making it visual, the impact is much stronger than words could ever be.

The Upside of Downside

Salesmen are encouraged to stay positive. I don't know why. I've always found that a vivid and scary description of what will happen to someone's business or job if they do nothing or continue on their present path can be really helpful when trying to persuade them to take a risk and try something new.

Doctors are great at this. They tell you that if you have surgery, there's a good possibility you'll feel better afterward. But when they tell you the downside, what's likely to happen if you don't have the surgery, that closes the deal.

I have a Hollywood screenwriter friend who says he knows that a studio executive is interested in buying a pitch when he or she asks, "Who else has seen this?" He knows that passing on a pitch that a competing studio turns into a hit movie can cost him his job. The same goes for clients.

We all know that advertising campaigns or communication strategies can cost millions to execute. For many companies and decisionmakers, the cost of approving something so expensive can be frightening. Saying yes can be terrifying. On the other hand, saying no doesn't seem to cost a thing. If you really want to sell your idea, then you've got to make them aware of the downside of thinking safe.

It's up to you to make no feel a lot more costly than yes. If the client feels the idea is too dangerous or risky, ask how she would feel if she woke up tomorrow and found out that a competitor had been willing to take the risk and has executed a similar idea. Have her imagine a world where she could no longer have the idea, and ask how she would feel then.

Sometimes the best way to be positive, or at least get a positive result, is to gently turn the conversation toward hellfire and brimstone.

They Didn't Come to See the Props

I can draw beautifully. When I first started presenting ideas for television commercials, I drew elaborate storyboards that looked like film strips—with wide shots, close-ups, well-rendered characters, and detailed product shots. They were little works of art.

But clients don't care about art, craft, effort, or how you got there. People who buy professional communications services, like ads, scripts, menu designs, or blog copy, want to see and hear what they want to sell, not what you made, thought of, or worked hard on.

I began to understand this when I was working for my first big client, Taco Bell. They had a system for approving advertising ideas that involved three different meetings. First, I would present my beautiful storyboards to the brand manager, the lowest-ranking person on the client's marketing team. If he liked the work, he'd invite his boss into the room, and I would present to her. If the two of them liked the work, they would invite me to pitch to the vice president of Marketing. That was the system. To sell an idea, I had to perform three shows back-to-back.

I spent days drawing beautiful storyboards. Then because I was so proud of my idea, I just turned my beautiful storyboards around and showed them to the young brand manager, expecting him to examine each gorgeous frame and see just how terrific the idea was.

I sat there holding the boards inches from his nose so he could see every detail. He looked at them as though he was reading a comic strip, and as he got to the end, he said he liked the idea and called his boss in. When the head of advertising came in, I did the same thing again. I flipped over the boards and let her study them. She did, and went to get the vice president of Marketing.

Between meetings, my boss, who was sitting next to me the whole time, leaned over and whispered, "You have the idea. Stop presenting the storyboards and make them see the commercial, or you're going to lose it."

When the vice president of Marketing—the one whose opinion mattered most—arrived, I left the boards face-down on the table and acted out the commercial. I set the scene and described the camera movements. I explained what was in the wide shots and how the camera would caress the product in close-ups. I played all the characters and did all the sound effects. In other words, I showed him the commercial instead of the boards. He bought it.

All this time, I had been hiding behind my pretty storyboards. They were nice, but they were not what the clients had come to the meeting to see or buy. They wanted to see their commercials, not my boards. I just needed to be reminded to sell what the people buying wanted to buy, not the props I was good at making.

You Are the Solution— Not the Problem; Act Like It

When I was in elementary school, I was smart but a slow reader and a poor student. My report cards always said, "Josh is not working up to his potential." I saw myself as a disappointment.

Early in my career, I went into presentations assuming that my ideas would disappoint. Regardless of the quality of my work, I always pictured the meeting going the same way. I would walk in and unpack my comps or storyboards. My boss or client would be sitting respectfully at a conference table. I would flip over the boards, present my stuff, and stand there for a beat as my pitiful little ideas hung in the air as appreciated as a fart in a space suit. Then my boss or client would issue a disappointed sigh and say, "What else you got?" I'd say, "That's it. That's all I have. Can I have more time?" The boss or client would say, "No. We're out of time, and now we've got nothing."

Then I heard a story about General Ulysses S. Grant that made me reconsider what I expected from myself.

It seemed that General Grant was terribly afraid of going into battle. He could only face the enemy by getting drunk the night before. One day Grant and his army pitched camp opposite a Rebel army that they planned to face on the battlefield the following morning. As usual, Grant was afraid. And as usual, he got drunk. But when Grant woke up the next morning, expecting to do battle, he found that the Rebel army had disappeared. He walked through their encampment, saw tents and bedrolls and empty pairs of shoes. He also noticed frying pans and coffeepots still cooking on campfires. Grant could tell that whoever was just there had taken off in a hurry. Walking through that abandoned encampment, he realized that his opposing general was just as afraid of doing battle with Grant as Grant was of doing battle with him.

That story forever changed how I viewed presenting. The people I present to are as afraid as I am that I don't have a good idea, and realizing that made me a very persuasive presenter. After all, if they had any idea what to do, they'd do it themselves.

Before, I would think to myself, *My clients have MBAs, work at big companies with big advertising budgets. Who the hell am I, some twenty-six-year-old kid from art school, to tell them what to do?* Now my thinking had shifted to, *I am the best hope these guys have. They're praying I have a good idea. All I have to do is walk in and let them know their prayers have been answered.*

I no longer saw bosses or clients as authority figures who looked at my work and deemed it right or wrong, exciting or disappointing. I saw people just waiting for me to walk in with an idea that would make their fear and anxiety go away. So that's what I would do.

What Have They Got to Lose?

In any collaborative effort, you will deal with different people who have different skills and are motivated by different things. In order to succeed in a collaboration, you must know what's motivating the people you're working with. Sometimes they'll tell you. Sometimes they won't.

Once, I was shooting a television commercial and the film got damaged. The bath that was supposed to dissolve a layer of emulsion from one side of the film was the wrong temperature and every roll of film ended up looking as if it had been shot in a snowstorm. A meeting was called to decide what to do. Could we use any of the film we shot? Could we take these scenes out of the commercial? Should we reshoot them?

There were half a dozen people in the room when we screened the footage. One guy over in the corner, an older gentleman, couldn't seem to see any problem at all. At the end of every scene, he would yell something to the effect of "That was a nice piece" or "You only need a second, right?" I could not figure out why the oldest, most experienced filmmaker in the room was having trouble seeing that every inch of film was bad, every frame useless. Then it dawned on me that he was the guy who was financially responsible. If the rest of us decided to reshoot, the money would be coming out of his pocket. At that meeting, I learned what it meant to be an executive producer. It was great preparation for working on *Mad Men*.

When I got hired out of art school, all the people wearing suits looked and sounded the same to me. But they weren't the same at all. Some of them were clients. It was their money we were talking about spending. Some of the suits were account people. They were the ones who had to manage the client's money and expectations. Some were research people; others, media buyers. At first, I didn't understand what each of these different people had to gain or lose as a result of a meeting. So I kept my mouth shut. As I listened, I tried to figure out who was going to say what next. I discovered that not everybody is motivated by money. Not everybody is motivated by the quality of the work. Not everybody has a hidden agenda. But everybody in the meeting is motivated by something. It's always helpful to know what people want. It's helpful to know what they absolutely *don't* want, too.

Be Willing to Walk Away a Winner

My wife's grandfather used to run casinos in Las Vegas. He said that the difference between winners and losers is that a winner is willing to walk away a winner. A loser keeps playing until he has lost.

Hard as it is to believe, I've seen people who would rather keep talking and go through every idea they've brought into a presentation than stand up and leave halfway through with the yes that they came for.

We all have friends who come back from Las Vegas with the same story. "I was up $500. I was up $1,000. I was up $2,000. Then I lost it all." The story is about how their luck changed, as if their choices had nothing to do with it.

Winning and losing in business often has a good deal to do with how people see themselves and their lot in the world. Some see themselves as winners and are willing to pick up the chips when they're ahead and walk away from the table. Those who feel deep down that they are losers will play until their suspicions are confirmed.

Most creative people are hardwired to spend a lot of time planning for the worst. We rehearse arguments. We have contingency plans we keep in the bag, just in case. We go over time and again what to do if things go wrong. Worst of all, we tend to ignore the possibility that things may go completely our way.

I'm not saying things will go right if you just think positively and act like a winner. I'm saying, if and when things do go right and you get a yes, stop talking, stop selling, stop seducing, stop doing everything you're doing. Just get up, shake hands, and walk away a winner.

Final Thoughts on Presenting

Check your fly.
Check your teeth.
Check your nose.

I've seen it happen. Enough said.

Part Four
The Secret Story
of Online Seduction

A Medium Message

In 1964, philosopher Marshall McLuhan wrote, "The medium is the message." Huh?

According to the McLuhan website, he meant that "each medium, independent of the content it mediates, has its own intrinsic effects which are its unique message." Again, huh? I worked in advertising for years and had never understood what McLuhan meant until I began working on *Mad Men* and learned how things were done on Madison Avenue during the early 1960s.

In the days of "Mad men," successful communicators realized that, in addition to the product they were selling, the medium they advertised it on had its own unique message—or *intrinsic effect*.

When advertisers or their agencies bought media space and time to advertise their products and services, they also bought that intrinsic effect. For example, when advertisers bought an outdoor campaign from their agency, they were buying a medium that was great for introducing new products and making people curious to know more. Advertisers knew that in order to be successful, the type of ad had to take advantage of the medium, so the smart ones would first decide what kind of business result they wanted. Local newspapers are great for limited-time offers and making people feel a sense of urgency. Magazines are the perfect place to show people what makes a product, service, or idea different. In the "Mad men" days, different media were appropriate for different messages, and different messages led to expectations of different business results.

One reason the intrinsic effect of online media is tricky to figure out is because the Internet is not owned or operated by media companies. It's owned and operated by the people who use it for their own collection of personal benefits. So what the Internet is *intrinsically* good at doing is different for every person using it to do something. When millions of different people are using online New Media to do millions of different things, it's difficult for advertisers to identify what kind of business results they should expect when they advertise online.

People online are the masters of their own universe. Unlike traditional media audiences, Internet users have actively participated in building their own networks. They paid for the network, hooked it up, and uploaded, posted, friended, and added to it one node—or connection—at a time.

The personal, self-programmed nature of the Internet means that its inherent effect goes beyond what is possible to sell. The unique message of the Internet is that the possibilities of what users can learn, master, create, share, build, and *become* are limitless.

Building Babel
One Bit at a Time

I've said it before, but I think it's worth repeating. There are four realistic business goals companies can hope to achieve through advertising:

1. Increase inquiries by making people curious.
2. Boost sales by giving customers temporary opportunities or limited-time offers.
3. Improve market share or get a bigger piece of the pie by reminding people what makes the company or its products and services special.
4. Build or defend profit margins by aligning the company's philosophy or reason for being with its customer's philosophy or reason for being.

From an advertising point of view, what Marshall McLuhan meant by "the medium is the message" is that each of the many different media options available back in 1964 was well suited by its very nature to achieving one of these goals. Following are examples of the business goals in action. There can be mixing and matching of goals and media, but these were the original starting places.

Outdoor posters and billboards are all about what's new. The very nature of outdoor advertising makes people curious. By providing contrast to the landscape, posters and billboards have an inherently novel effect. And the larger-than-life quality of outdoor practically screams, "Check it out. Here inside this frame is something new and different!" Inquiries are increased when curiosity is incited in this way.

Local newspaper, radio, and TV are all about immediate opportunity. Nothing tops these vehicles as a way to impart a sense of urgency. Different types of local media, for instance, are great for delivering information about a temporary, nearby opportunity or close, impending danger, such as storms or road closings. They are also highly effective if you're a retailer who needs to move some merchandise. Announce the sale you're having in newspaper ads, or shout about it on local radio. The immediacy of local newspaper, radio, and TV makes their intrinsic effect a temporary bump in traffic or sales.

National magazines are about different strokes for different folks. National print magazines are effective for making people familiar with memorable differences among products and services—and their intrinsic effect is increasing market share. The specific natures of *Road and Track, Better Homes and Gardens, Vogue, Esquire,* and other national magazines are ideal for helping advertisers compare and critique the philosophies, features, craftsmanship, or execution that separate one company, product, service, or idea from another in a particular category. Want to woo customers away from your rivals and build market share? Start with a new tagline that clearly states a unique promise to the market and demonstrate that difference over and over again with a series of four-color magazine spreads that make the competition look lame by comparison.

National television broadcasts help build profit margins by aligning a sponsor's philosophy with a viewing household's values. Back in the day, before subscription-paid cable television, broadcast sponsors thought of network programs and personalities as guests sent into the homes of their customers to inform and entertain. Everything about national broadcast programming and national advertising was designed to reinforce the idea of shared values, national outlook, and mutual love and respect. The intrinsic message of nationally broadcast television is that all of us—you at home, the network broadcaster, and we the sponsor—all share the same values. We all appreciate the same stuff. Cable networks, however, are like private clubs. The relationship between network, advertiser, and audience is basically the same but reinforced by an added insider/outsider aspect. "It's not TV. It's HBO."

In the "Mad men" days—and even beyond them—once an advertising agency and client agreed on the client's business goal, determining which medium would deliver the desired results was purely academic. Say a client walked into a Madison Avenue ad agency in 1964 with a four-year plan to build his brand. The agency account executive might have scribbled out the following business and media plan:

Year 1: Increase inquiries/generate leads. Yellow Pages, outdoor posters/billboards. In terms of media strategy, when a product is new it's impossible to know exactly who the target audience will be, so it makes sense to cast the net as wide as you can by using open and ubiquitous media. Up till now, this included outdoor billboards, posters, and transit advertising. Billboards and posters are not what anyone would call "targeted." Outdoor media expose a message to everyone who passes by regardless of whether or not they're open to the posted proposition.

Year 2: Grow sales. Continue with outdoor posters/billboards; add local newspaper and radio promotions.

Year 3: Improve market share. Freshen outdoor posters/billboards; roll out magazine ads.

Year 4: Build profit margins. Print, print, print, plus network TV sponsorship.

The account exec would distribute this media plan to the research, media, and creative departments, and teams would get to work researching customers and competitors, pricing outdoor media in the client's most active markets, and creating concepts suitable for posters and billboards.

In the "medium is the message" world, the people creating and managing messages understood the intrinsic effects of the various media at their disposal——and knew how to use them.

Advertising giants of traditional old-school media like William Bernbach, George Lois, and Mary Wells Lawrence knew from years of experience the intrinsic effects of different media—and therefore had confidence in the business results they, and their clients, could expect from the ads they created.

Knowing this is important in the Information Age because when people use the word *banner* today, they're not talking about a painted canvas hanging in an outdoor venue. They're talking about a group of pixels embedded in a webpage that's linked to an advertiser. The advertiser's intention when buying online banner ads is to increase inquiries about a product or service. That's why the banner links through to the advertiser's website. But just because the message sender's intended result of buying online banners is the same as when buying traditional real-world banners and posters, *the intrinsic effects of the two media on the message receiver may not be the same at all*. People have very different relationships with outdoor posters and ads than they have with webpages and pop-ups that appear on their personal computer networks and smartphones. Just because someone decided to use the same word to describe two very different things is no reason to believe that people will respond in the same way to messages sent via these two very different media. Before deciding on what media best complement and support your particular message, identify—as best as you can—how and why a person is interactacting with that medium in the first place.

Before deciding on what media best support your message, identify how and why a person is interacting with that medium.

The Mission of Mini Media Moguls

Want to watch TV? Just buy a TV, plug it in, and turn it on. In a couple of seconds, you are watching sponsored programs—entertainment or news shows someone else has paid to produce, schedule, and send over the airwaves to your new TV.

Want online media? That's a different story. First you need to buy some computer hardware. Then you have to sign up with an Internet service provider (ISP) who will take the ones and zeros–that digital information that together makes up the stuff you want to read, listen to, watch, or surf—and send it through a cable or bounce it off a satellite and into your home. Then you need to choose a browser that can put all those bits back together into stuff that looks like pages, sounds like music, or plays like video. If you want to watch a movie, you have to sub-scribe to another service, such as Netflix. If you manage to get all the pieces working right, congratulations! You are now running a digital mini media network. You've got hardware working with software, plus an ISP feeding you digital pages, programs, and applications.

No single person, business, or organization invented or built the Internet. It's been made, paid for, owned, and operated by the people and companies who want it, bought the hardware and software to build it, and connected their hardware and software to the whole big network. Users can send, store, text, tweet, upload, search, see, learn, buy, comment, and connect with anyone, anytime, anywhere. Time and space do not exist online, making the Internet—and its possibilities—boundless.

One big difference between traditional media and digital online media is that, when you're online you are not passively absorbing a linear narrative of someone else's making. You are watching, reading, and listening for sure. But you are also gaming, blogging, posting, collaborating, editing, and curating your experience—your story—on a network that *you* have created.

As the creator of your own mini media network, when you are online you are doing, on a small scale, exactly what the head of NBC does on a very large one. When you use Netflix, you are paying movie producers like NBC does. When you pay the ISP, you are paying to have the movie you bought from Netflix broken up into bits and distributed to your hardware, just as NBC had to pay the government to license the TV spectrum over which they distribute a signal. Click here or there to decide what will play when on your network, and you're selecting the programs for the audience—you. In other words, you are in control of your network.

Naturally, it stands to reason that your relationship with something you paid for and operate—like your own digital network—is going to be different from your relationship to something given to you ostensibly for free, like sponsored television. You have more time and money

> Time and space do not exist online, making the Internet—and its possibilities—boundless.

The owner-operator nature of the Internet makes the intrinsic effect of online digital media more about the personal journey of each individual user.

invested in your network. It's yours and it's personal. Unlike traditional advertising and other types of persuasion aimed at people in general, online digital media is much more about *you* and your own unique possibilities.

The Internet is like a place where we are all alone together. The Internet's boundless possibilities and the owner-operator nature of its existence make the intrinsic effect of online digital media more about the personal journey of each individual user than about the collective shared experience of everyone being online together.

Metcalfe's Law

People who pay for, build, and operate their own media networks expect to grow their networks, program their networks, and control their networks. Building, owning, and operating a network costs money, but growing a personal network can also create value.

According to Ethernet co-inventor Robert Metcalfe, the value of a network increases exponentially with the addition of every new node. A node is any point on a network. It can be a person like a Facebook friend, a place like a web address, a file like an MP3 of a song, or JPG image.

When people pay for and build a digital network in order to get online, it doesn't take long before they start adding nodes to expand their networks. This is Metcalfe's Law at work, and it explains why early Internet users used Napster to add music to their new little digital networks. It also explains why people add Facebook friends who are not real friends to their digital networks. More nodes theoretically equal more value.

In real-world economics, value is derived from scarcity. Metcalfe's law is important because it explains why economic value on network-based systems is derived from

What
people
need to do
online is
write and
share their
own stories.

just the opposite: ubiquity. The more nodes you have, the more valuable your network. One copy of Microsoft Word is not very valuable to Microsoft. A large network of Word users is.

Building a social network of friends, fans, and followers online is like a network TV show building an audience. It's not the show itself that has value. The value of a TV show to a network is measured by the show's ability to attract an audience. The network makes money by selling advertisers (or other networks) access to the show's big audience.

Kim Kardashian has no value as an informer or entertainer. She doesn't actually inform or act. Even so, she has around three million Twitter followers. Her value is derived from her large audience, and advertisers pay her to gain entrée to that audience. Kim is nice to know about, but what people *need* to do online is write and share their own stories.

Techno Trekkers:
Four Stories of One Hero

I was in a Paris stationery store buying some pens and writing paper for my two daughters. The shopkeeper and I were having a polite conversation about the paper I was buying and how it has been made the same way in the same Italian mill for six hundred years.

When she asked what I did for a living, the conversation went from polite to tense. I said, "I went to art school, where I was trained as a painter and printmaker. Then I became an advertising art director and I made TV commercials. Now I'm a co-producer on a TV show. And when I go home to Los Angeles, I'm going to write a book." The shopkeeper became irate and said, "This could never happen in France. Here, you are what you are, and you do what you do. And that's it."

Her anger was not directed at me. It was directed at France. But it made me realize how I often take for granted the thing that really makes Americans different from the other people in the world.

Americans are constantly changing, evolving, and trying to better our lot. The pursuit of happiness is in our DNA and to find happiness, we either change our surroundings—"Go west, young man"—or we try to change ourselves—à la *How to Win Friends and Influence People.*

Americans change so much and so often that sometimes we don't even realize we're doing it, especially online. The desire to change and improve ourselves is a very big part of why we spend so much time online.

American consumers are on a personal journey trying to get from their "selves," or who they think they are, to their "ideal selves," or who they want to be. People buy products and services and use media that help them close the gap, and get them closer to who they want to be.

I don't think people really "surf" the Internet. Surfing implies that they are bobbing around on waves of information and not really getting anywhere. When I try to find a metaphor for what people are doing online, I picture a scene from a Bugs Bunny cartoon in which a train is chasing him down the track. As the train bears down, the track runs out, and Bugs starts laying track as fast as he can in front of himself and the oncoming train. When we're online, everything we do, every click on a hyperlink, every new page we land on, every picture we post, every comment we make, article we read, or message we send is like laying another length of track in front of a moving train.

Online, people have some sense of what's motivating them—that's the train—but they are laying track down as they click their way around from one digital media experience to another. I think of these folks who are online and simultaneously on their journey to their ideal selves as Techno Trekkers.

> People buy products and services and use media that help them close the gap, and get them closer to who they want to be.

Techno Trekkers are picking up and putting down four kinds of stories as they journey from their current self—who they are—to their ideal self—who they want to be.

Need-to-know stories are the primary and most important of the four types. They let Techno Trekkers define their ideal selves by revealing what's possible. A musician might start her day by reading *Rolling Stone* online. A construction worker might wake up to the local weather report on the radio. Say we're talking about a person in the world of media and entertainment who views herself as an artist, writer, or businessperson; her need-to-know stories are likely to be found in the *New York Times, Variety, Adweek*, or on *Deadline Hollywood*. Rupert Murdoch knows that a person in business reads the *Wall Street Journal* because if you are going to think of yourself as a businessperson, you need to know what is possible to achieve in business. When Murdoch bought the *WSJ*, he put up a pay wall on the website, because he knew instinctively that need-to-know stories are the only stories Techno Trekkers or anyone will pay for online.

Nice-to-know stories are much more about probability than possibility. They're stories about what kinds of behavior, relationships, and actions are *likely* to result in different outcomes. It's nice to know about any opportunities out there to be had. Nice-to-know stories are usually advertising-supported and found for free on aggregator sites like *Huffington Post*, blogs, and sponsored websites. The stories are nice because they help with information—including information about products and services—that may be useful on a Techno Trekker's journey to what's possible. They inform about things that can speed a person's path from here to there.

Techno Trekkers are picking up and putting down four kinds of stories as they journey from their current self—who they are—to their ideal self—who they want to be.

Nice-to-say stories. These include updates on Facebook or Twitter and let a Trekker's friends, family, and others know how their journey is progressing. What are they seeing? What they are thinking? How's it going? How is the Trekker's social status changing? Nice-to-say stories are all about what's going on in the Trekker's life—where they are now or how their life has changed recently. Facebook, for example, is built around the "update status" entry bar.

Need-to-say stories. These stories tend to be narratives about dumping baggage. They are similar to the idea of confession, or the postcards seen on the website PostSecret. Need-to-say stories are about people or things Techno Trekkers are done with and no longer want to be burdened by. These stories belong to the old selves Trekkers will no longer be when they become their new ideal selves.

A friend of mine was building an online site for a big company that sold groceries like cookies and frozen food. As a way of getting homemakers involved in the site, he asked moms to anonymously post stories about the worst thing they ever did as a mother. In a couple of weeks people had posted some forty thousand stories about letting their kids eat Popsicles for breakfast in the car on the way to school. This is an example of a need-to-say story, all about the stuff the women could no longer carry around if they were ever going to be able to think of themselves as good moms. These stories are confessional by nature and tend to work best when put on a site with thousands of others just like them so the people who share them can see they are not alone and don't feel so bad.

For persuaders, the thing to remember is that in offline traditional media advertising stories, the product

Messages about products and services are appreciated only to the extent that they support and advance the story of the hero.

or service is the hero that makes people's lives better. But in online digital and social media, customers are the heroes of their own stories. And messages about products and services are appreciated only to the extent that they support and advance the story of the hero.

Excuse Me, Would You Please Get Out of My Movie?

The saying "It's all about the journey" is truer than ever online. We're charting our course with need-to-know stories that help provide a vision of what it's possible to be or do. We're navigating our way with nice-to-know stories that show us how to improve our odds of succeeding under particular circumstances. We're letting people know how we're progressing on our journey through nice-to-say stories and updates. Or we're getting rid of excess baggage through the confessional nature of need-to-say stories.

Just as the motivations of online media users—Techno Trekkers—are different from those of offline customers, so are the questions we should ask before trying to seduce them.

As I mentioned earlier, unlike the intrinsic effects of traditional media, the inherent benefit of the Internet is different for every person using it. That means the questions regarding your audience need to be completely reframed. Offline advertising messages are designed to show a single hero product or service answering one of four consumer questions: What is it? Why now? What's different about it? And who else thinks it's good? Online— where the customers are the hero—persuaders should consider four different consumer questions before placing messages in an online environment:

- Does this change what I think is possible?
- Does this change what I think is probable?
- Does this change my status or position within my network and, if so, who should know about it?
- Does this help me leave what I want to leave behind?

The secret of online seduction is knowing where you fit into a Techno Trekker's journey—or story—and how your product or service can help advance their cause.

For example, nice-to-know stories are about improving a person's odds of succeeding under particular circumstances, and advertisers and persuaders are welcome to contribute relevant information and opportunities. E-Trade is a natural for sponsoring a retirement website because they offer services that can potentially help people reach this particular goal faster. Likewise, most people are open to Marriott advertising hotel deals to go along with the flight you just booked.

One of the problems today's advertisers and persuaders are having online is that after years of being told that the best way to persuade the public is by making ads or stories that show "the product as hero," advertisers are having to adjust to putting their products in supporting roles in stories about other heroes.

> Just as the motivations of online media users are different from those of offline customers, so are the questions we should ask before trying to seduce them.

Anyone who's sat in a movie theater and listened to the audience boo their way through the commercials shown before the coming attractions can appreciate what I'm saying about being in the right place with the right intent. If you're a persuader who's not willing to accept a supporting role in the online world, now would be a good time to kindly excuse yourself and get out of the picture.

Going Viral Is the Internet Applauding a New Possibility

When people viewing a story together in public agree that what they are seeing or hearing represents a new possibility, they applaud.

Applause is a message sent to a performer from a member of the audience. That message is "Nice job redefining what I thought was possible. Well done, you!" Applause is also a message sent to and from one audience member to another. The message to the other members of the audience is "We all agree that what we are seeing and hearing is redefining what we all thought possible. Right? Right."

A guitar solo can, in twelve bars, redefine for an audience the depth of feeling they thought was possible for a person to express with a guitar. So they applaud. A kid's poem read aloud at a school performance can change what grown-ups think is possible for a child to perceive and put into words. So they applaud.

The Internet is where we are both a network of owner-operators and audience members who are alone, yet

What goes viral is something that changes, redefines, or expands some group's idea about what's possible.

connected. And "going viral" is how people online applaud a new possibility.

We check our reaction to seeing something we didn't know was possible by reaching out to our network of family and friends and saying to everyone to whom we are connected, "Look at this. I didn't know this was possible. Did you know this was possible? I had no idea it was possible for one person to dance in so many different ways! Did you? I didn't know it was possible for a cat to talk! Did you? I didn't know it was possible for a kid to play the piano like that! Did you?"

What goes viral is something that changes, redefines, or expands some group's idea about what's possible.

Recently a Heineken ad campaign that went viral offered to send people anywhere they wanted to go in the world but only if they agreed to go now. Who imagined it was possible for a beer company to run an ad for something that was exciting and fun and not about beer?

Before the summer of 2014, did anyone ever consider it possible to fight ALS (Lou Gehrig's disease) by dumping ice water on your head? But it happened during a Facebook challenge that raised donations totaling more than $100 million.

Cool, funny, cute, and painful doesn't do it. When creating messages that you would like to go viral—or get passed around free of charge on a network owned and operated by other people—try asking a member of your intended audience if the story or video or ad changes their notion of what's *possible*. If what you've got is more death defying, faster, more profound, cooler, funnier, cuter, more painful, or weirder than someone thinks or thought possible, your message is on its way. If it's not, it's not going anywhere.

Captains of Empathy

Successful advertisers are the ones who can be both public champions of products and services and private captains of empathy.

Empathy is about understanding what people are doing and why. People are using the online networks they build to write and distribute the stories of their lives. By watching a YouTube clip, for instance, the user is either programming or perusing their own network. They are *doing* something. And they are doing it for a reason. And their reasons matter to an advertising message.

Persuading in the physical world is getting someone somewhere to do something. Persuading in the online world is getting someone who's already doing something to do something *else*.

To help people find new possibilities, persuaders need to entertain, enthrall, and inspire.

To help people understand new probabilities, persuaders need to inform.

To help people track their progress, persuaders need to support them in their efforts and help these people connect to others who are on a similar path.

To help people change, persuaders need to let them leave who they were and what they did behind.

Persuading
in the
online
world
means
getting
someone
who's
already
doing
something
to do
something
else.

Instead of the traditional "What is the product?" "Who is it for?" and "What makes it different?" we need to be asking something completely different: "Where are my customers? Who do they dream of becoming? How can we help?" And perhaps most important: "How will the story about my products improve my customers' odds of becoming who they want to be?"

A Trout, a Swiss Army Knife, an iPad, and YouTube

To reiterate the question raised by Lee Clow in the introduction: How *do* we use all these New Media opportunities?

Fifteen years ago I heard Bill Gates talk about the Internet and New Media. At the time people were using the phrase *Information Superhighway* to describe the network that was fast taking shape. Gates said that the metaphor was okay, so long as you understood that you were not going anywhere on the Superhighway. His description of being on the Internet was more like standing in the middle of a twelve-lane boulevard with everything that ever is, was, or will be racing toward you at the speed of light. This idea significantly shaped my understanding of how advertising and New Media should work.

Online, the user is in active control of their online experience. Unlike traditional advertising audiences who

Online media's intrinsic effect is this: You get closer to what you want with every click.

tend to passively receive messages, online users *do* something in order to experience every word, picture, story, music file, or video.

Everything you choose to see combines to make New Media's intrinsic effect or unique message this: You get closer to what you want with every click.

For example, Google gets you one click closer to what you are searching for. Facebook gets you one click closer to who you want to be or be with. Amazon gets you one click closer to what you want to have. Big, full-service web browsers like Safari or Firefox are a little like the local bus, bringing you closer to the stuff you want but dragging along with it a lot of other stuff like page takeovers and pop-ups that you may not be interested in. And apps are like little speedy express trains, getting you closer to what you want faster and easier—without all the added noise and baggage.

Offline, the product or service is hero. For decades Procter & Gamble insisted that their brand managers answer three questions before creating advertising or buying traditional media: What is the product? Who is it for? How is it different from the competition?

Online, the user is hero. The question every hero wants answered before doing something is "What good will I do myself, my family, or my community if I take this action?" This makes the nature of the three questions marketers, advertisers, and message makers need to ask before creating advertising for New Media totally different. Before posting any ad or banner or buying any search engine optimization program or "viral" video online, the questions need to be "Who is my customer?" "What person, place, or thing are they trying to get closer to?" and "How will this help them?"

A couple of years ago my wife and I went to Mammoth Lake in the Sierra Nevada to go fishing. I had not been fishing in more than thirty-five years, and my wife never had. But it was a warm July day and spending a couple hours out on the lake in a boat seemed like a great idea. As luck would have it, we caught a beautiful twelve-inch trout, which I wanted to clean, bone, and cook. However, I had no idea how to do any of it. So we went back to the condo, where we had a Wi-Fi connection.

I had a twelve-inch trout, a Wi-Fi connection to the Internet, and an iPad. And because I was going to the Sierra Nevada, I had a Swiss Army knife that my mom and dad gave me when I was eleven.

I went online and started searching for how to clean a fish. Now, the name of my Swiss Army knife is the Fisherman. So I checked the Swiss Army knife site, figuring that there would be some information there explaining how to use it. I didn't find any. I then decided to check the websites of other camping products and brands I knew and trusted, like Buck Knives and Coleman. Again, no luck. Then I went on YouTube and typed in "how to clean a fish." What a bonanza. There were all sorts of anglers and guys with different methods for cleaning trout. Some were much better filmmakers than others. Some methods seemed easy and quick, while others looked like a royal pain in the ass. A guy with a red shirt had a method whereby you made a couple of slits with a very sharp knife under the fish's mouth then stuck your thumb and finger in and pulled everything out with one quick, determined motion. It worked perfectly. In about ten minutes, with the help of a Wi-Fi connection, an iPad, a Swiss Army knife, YouTube, and some guy in a red shirt, I had cleaned, boned, and cooked my fish.

"Who is my customer?" "What person, place, or thing are they trying to get closer to?" and "How will this help them?"

The thing I wanted to get closer to was a clean, boned, and cooked trout. I went online expecting to get help from international brands I grew up with, knew, and trusted—and got nothing. Instead, I was helped by a random fisherman on YouTube. For those international brands with access to Big Data, big production dollars, and good message makers, my trout and I were a missed New Media opportunity. If advertisers are wondering where in the world to be online, this example should give them one good idea. When Victorinox Swiss Army puts up a website and sells knives called the Fisherman or the Angler, they should anticipate being visited by people who have a fish problem. A good knife solves part of the fish problem. But a good brand solves as much of the fish problem as it can.

Today even experienced marketers are hung up on the technological part of the New Media problem. Many of them find it confusing. But they don't need to understand how the technology works in order to discern the relationship between their business goals and the creative messages they need to create in order to achieve them. Just like successful offline marketing, advertisers and message makers need to know the customer. As long as advertisers can decide what business goal they want to achieve, messages can be still be made that will provoke online users to act based on curiosity, a sense of urgency, a sense of trust in familiar types of products, or a sense of trust in familiar types of people.

When I hear people talk about Big Data and research companies or organizations monitoring what people do online, I get the sense that they don't understand what makes Big Data different from other research. It's simply that Big Data figures out what person, place, thing, or action an online user is trying to get closer to. Once you know that, it's up to you to determine where and how your product or service fits in.

Right now Amazon is using information gleaned from Big Data to move products physically closer to the people who are likely to be buying them. For instance, if you have repeatedly searched for information on Alexander the Great, Amazon will make sure they move that DVD or book to a warehouse closer to you so it's ready and waiting to be quickly delivered.

At the end of *Confessions of an Advertising Man*, David Ogilvy offers some sage advice to young people starting their careers in advertising agencies. He recommends that you pick a subject about which your agency knows too little, and become an authority on it. He suggests studying subjects like "the psychology of retail pricing, advertising budgets, and international brand strategy. . . . Once you become the acknowledged authority on any of these troublesome subjects, you will be able to write your own ticket."

In an attempt to update his advice for today's generation of message makers, my advice is to embed yourself in a *community* that your employer knows little or nothing about. It's great if the group is relevant to the future success of the company for whom you are working. It's even better if it's a group in which you are truly interested and involved. Learn something intimate about the group that Big Data can't know. Find out what makes them smile, tear up, or get out of bed in the morning. Get to know a group of customers or would-be customers inside and out, online and offline, here, there, and everywhere. Know them like you know the back of your hand, your family, or your favorite movie. Succeeding in the information economy takes skills, imagination, and *insider information*.

Succeeding in the information economy takes skills, imagination, and *insider information.*

So the next time you're in a Starbucks trying to come up with a persuasive message for some offline, online, social media, or New Media audience and you're feeling guilty for wasting time checking your email or hanging out on your Facebook page or poking around on the Internet, don't worry. As long as you keep searching for the ways that the words, pictures, stories, music, product, service, experience, or event you're persuading with can in some way help the people to whom you are connected, relax. You are doing the job. Like Bill Gates said about the Internet: It will come to you.

Acknowledgments

I want to acknowledge and thank Chris Boutée. She helped me organize my ideas and write and edit each essay. And I could not have completed this book without her help and hard work.

I also want to thank Robert Myman, Jenn Joel, Mary Ellen O'Neill, and everyone at Workman Publishing who helped make this book happen.

Special thanks to Matt Weiner for giving me the opportunity to work on *Mad Men*—where I got to think long and hard about what I saw, learned, and did while working in advertising agencies and also where I got to contribute to the writing and crafting of one of the greatest American stories ever told.

I want to acknowledge other people with whom I worked on *Mad Men*: Scott Hornbacher, Dan Bishop, and Christopher Brown and especially my trusted friend, rabbi, and cohort Bob Levinson, the show's other advertising consultant.

I also need to acknowledge some of the *Mad Men* writers and producers who were particularly patient and encouraging with me as I learned to express and articulate my ideas about business and advertising. Thank you, Lisa Albert, Robin Veith, Kater Gordon, Brett Johnson, Jonathan Igla, Andre and Maria Jacquemetton, Semi Chellas, David Isaacs, Janet Leahy, Carly Wray, Victor Levin, Erin Levy, Allison Mann, Tom Palmer, Frank Pierson, Chris Provenzano, Tom Smuts, Mike Saltzman, Dahvi Waller, and Robert Towne.

Thanks to the actors who made the job of using words, pictures, stories, and music to make someone, somewhere *do* something look like a smart, cool, and sexy way to make a living: Jon Hamm, Elisabeth Moss, John Slattery, Christina Hendricks, Vincent Kartheiser, January Jones, Kiernan Shipka, Jessica Paré, Robert Morse, Rich Sommer, Aaron Staton, Jared Harris, Jay R. Ferguson, Bryan Batt, Michael Gladis, Ben Feldman, Kevin Rahm, and the rest of the cast of *Mad Men*.

Advertising is a collaborative art. I want to acknowledge and thank the creative people with whom I've worked developing strategies, ads, and campaigns. Without the help of the following people I would not have much advertising to talk about. Thank you, Jim Walker, Lisa Kleckner Ansis, Donna Portaro, Kathy Van Kerkhoven, Julie Clark Robinson, George Roux, Jeff Gelberg, Peter Andres, Tracy Davis, Bruce Dundore, Garry Sato, Brent Thomas, Chris Blum, Mark Vieha, Daniel Hainey, Robin Benson, Cliff Einstein, Julie Sandler, Howie Cohen, Mark Johnson, Joe Rein, Elissa Singstock, Sue Dawson, Julie Prendiville Roux, Mike Indgin, Geoff Katz, Savoy Hallinan, Jordin Mendelsohn, Richard Zien, Michelle Miller, Claudia Caplin, Kim Genkinger, Jeff Nee, Peter Darley Miller, Joe Pytka, Ken Gal, Chris Epting, Shari Cooper, Marnie Burns, Michael Bettendorf, David Angelo, Greg Collins, and Rich Siegel.

Last, I need to acknowledge my parents, Gershon and Tova Weltman, who encouraged my creativity and artistic disposition, and my children, Sophia and Gabrielle, who tolerate it.

About the Author

JOSH WELTMAN is a twenty-five-year veteran of the advertising business—a creative director, co-producer, writer, and artist. He has created commercials and ad campaigns for Taco Bell, Doritos, Carl's Jr., BMW, Microsoft, Whole Foods Market, Kia Motors, Green Burrito, and Cuties. He has authored everything from online guerrilla marketing efforts for small clients like Cirque Berzerk to national campaigns for global automotive companies like Kia Motors.

Josh Weltman has been involved with *Mad Men* since the show's first season. He worked closely with Matthew Weiner and the show's writers and producers to help ensure that *Mad Men* accurately depicted the process of creating ads and servicing clients and that the advertising and business stories played true to life, true to character, and true to the era. He also created most of the original ads seen on the show.

Josh graduated from Otis Institute of Art/Parsons School of Design with a BFA in Illustration and Communication Design and has been cited by the Cannes Lions International Festival of Creativity, the American Advertising Federation, and the Advertising Club of Los Angeles for excellence in his work. He and his wife, Angela Weltman, PhD, live in Los Angeles with their two daughters. *Seducing Strangers* is his first book.